RENEWING YOUR CHURCH
THROUGH HEALTHY SMALL GROUPS

Diana Curren Bennett

Foreword by Stephen A. Macchia

RENEWING YOUR CHURCH THROUGH HEALTHY SMALL GROUPS

INTENTIONAL RELATIONSHIPS FOR SPIRITUAL RENEWAL
8 WEEK TRAINING MANUAL FOR SMALL GROUP LEADERS

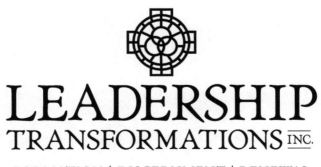

LEADERSHIP
TRANSFORMATIONS INC.

FORMATION | DISCERNMENT | RENEWAL

© 2016 by Diana Curren Bennett

Published by LTI Publications
P.O. Box 338, Lexington, MA 02420
www.leadershiptransformations.org

May 2016
Printed in the United States of America.

Library of Congress Cataloging-in-Publication Data
Bennett, Diana Curren, 1940 –
Renewing Your Church Through Healthy Small Groups / Diana Curren Bennett
ISBN 978-0692707265 (pbk.)
Religion / Christian Church / Leadership

Dedicated to those who yearn to see the church renewed

through caring and authentic small group communities

ACKNOWLEDGMENTS

During my years at Gordon-Conwell Theological Seminary, Dr. Richard Peace became an important mentor and encourager by challenging me in my passion for evangelism and discipleship. It is through his direction that I focused my ministry on the potential of creating healthy small groups for life-transformation. I am grateful.

I am also grateful for Dr. Garth Rosell and his guidance over many years at Gordon-Conwell as professor, advisor, Doctor of Ministry mentor, and friend. I am also most appreciative of Dr. Stephen Macchia, long-time ministry friend and co-worker, and also Doctor of Ministry mentor. I have been continually encouraged through his guidance.

I give thanks to the late Rev. David Midwood, my Doctor of Ministry project evaluator, to The Pilgrimage Training Group that provided my initial experiences of leading New England small group leadership training seminars, to my many friends and colleagues represented through the Leadership Network Forum for Small Group Directors, and to my New England Small Group Director co-workers who now gather yearly to share resources, creative ideas, and encouragement to one another as we commit to life-transforming ministry.

I am especially grateful to my editors, as without their expertise, many mistakes and vague explanations would have been left unnoticed. I thank Kara Rhoda, Eric Skytte, Jeff Schuliger, Lisa Forkner, Rick Anderson, and Peter Bennett more than they will ever comprehend!

And, of course, I thank my family. My husband, Peter, has contended with my times of excitement, the overwhelming challenges, high stress levels, never-ending deadlines, discouragements, and celebrations. I give him thanks for encouraging me during the hard times, challenging me in my presentations, and listening to my dilemmas.

Most importantly, I thank God for giving me new life, for continually guiding me through many years in my spiritual journey, and for His faithfulness in providing wisdom and stamina for a ministry that brings me great pleasure.

TABLE OF CONTENTS

CHAPTER 4
THE COVENANT: DESIGNING THE GROUP   61

CHAPTER 5
WORSHIP: FOCUSING ON GOD   87

CHAPTER 6
PREPARATION: UNLOCKING THE SCRIPTURES 109

CHAPTER 7
INTERACTION: CREATING EFFECTIVE DISCUSSION 133

CHAPTER 8
TROUBLESHOOTING: CONFLICT RESOLUTION   155

FOREWORD

To say that leadership makes a difference in the facilitation of a healthy small group experience is putting it mildly.

Leadership of a small group is not only essential but undeniably the most important ingredient to a healthy small group experience. Leaders either make or break a small group, depending on the very factors Diana Bennett outlines in this important book you are about to read.

I've been in small groups where it's painful to participate... where the pace of the time together is either too fast or too slow, when the content is either disregarded by ignoring or discrediting it, when the participants are allowed to either dominate the conversation or discourage fellow participants with unhelpful commentary, or when certain participants simply take over the leadership role by usurping or undermining the designated leader. I've also been in groups where the leader was either unqualified or simply flat and ineffective. Yes, leadership matters... and, more significantly, poor leadership always disrupts a small group.

I've also been privileged to participate in small groups where it's a joy to engage with each person around the circle and the leader does an excellent job of facilitating life-giving interaction. This is the small group experience when the time flies by, the group is engaging, no one is left out, and when it's fun to be together to pray, study, reflect, listen, and share at deeply meaningful levels. And it's this kind of small group experience that Diana Bennett wants you to have each time you meet.

Diana and I have served together in various ministry contexts for more than two decades. I've observed Diana in multiple settings and can attest to her vivacious spirit, intelligent mind, and hospitable gifts. She writes what she lives and her teaching herein will strengthen and equip you for leading a spiritually healthy group. Receive her counsel one morsel at a time and you'll discover that you are at the table of a veritable feast of wisdom for you and your small group.

God bless you abundantly as you listen with an attentive spirit and lead others with a servant's heart.

Your brother on the journey toward spiritual and relational health,

Stephen A. Macchia
Founder and President, Leadership Transformations, Inc.

INTRODUCTION

God changed the direction of my life through the experience of a healthy small group. For this reason, over the last twenty-five years, I have been actively challenging and training men, women, and young adults to learn the necessary personal character, tools, and concepts for creating healthy small group environments for personal and church renewal. Small groups are perfect venues for connecting people within the church family, for providing care, for encouraging personal spiritual growth, and for reaching out to others in the church and geographical community. The small group ministry is a strategic and necessary component of church life. Ministerial staff must support the formation and continual building of small groups for care, connection, and spiritual growth. The church family must hear support for healthy small groups from the pulpit and see by the modeling of these small groups that they are not a program, but a way of life.

It is important to understand what *healthy* implies. The term *unhealthy* and *healthy* will be referred to many times throughout the following chapters.

UNHEALTHY SMALL GROUPS

Why do people often respond negatively to the idea of becoming part of a small group? In my experience and from hearing situations from many people over the years, a small group is unhealthy when there is a lack of intentional leadership and where the leadership style resembles the laissez-faire attitude of "let it all just happen." This occurs when there is inadequate prayer and preparation, little understanding of the purpose for the time together, neglect in approaching the Scriptures with integrity, the inability to create effective discussion, no attention to the basic stages of growth in the life cycle of a small group, and little knowledge of how to deal with difficult personalities and the conflict that often surfaces. Unhealthy dynamics dominate and members are discouraged. In this unhealthy situation, the small group members do not make the small group a priority, the lack of trust level prevents intimacy and accountability, and the group flounders. Because authentic Christian community is lacking, the personal experience is less than inviting and certainly not a positive experience.

HEALTHY SMALL GROUP

When small groups are grounded in prayer and proper preparation, when they are well facilitated allowing ownership and high trust levels to develop, and when the members experience meaningful community, care and connection with God and one another, spiritual growth becomes evident, life-change happens, and strong disciples for Jesus Christ are developed. Spiritual renewal happens in healthy small groups!

HOW TO USE THIS MATERIAL

The purpose of this material is fourfold: (1) to cast a vision for creating authentic Christian community, (2) to assist pastors or directors of small group ministries with useful information for initial or on-going trainings, (3) to help individuals who desire to learn on their own, and (4) in particular, for a small group of potential leaders who desire to work through training material together. Anyone interested in leadership will find this resource a helpful tool for improving their understanding of the healthy basics for leading small groups that offer care, connection, and the challenge for spiritual growth and renewal.

There are many formats for delivering small group leadership training. Often churches rush into forming small group ministries by gathering a group of leaders and quickly starting the ministry in order to expedite the offering of small groups. I would, however, recommend that churches *hurry slowly* and train a few selected leaders over a period of time. Exposing new leaders and providing an environment where they can experience the skills and challenges of leadership as a group help produce more confident leaders. Working through a small group training such as the following will encourage, model, and explore various aspects of creating authentic Christian community through the small group arena itself. These training groups should meet together for eight weeks as a small group of potential leaders, experiencing and evaluating the various concepts and skills for creating healthy small group environments. The training group can be led by a pastor, teaching elder, director of small groups, or an experienced small group leader. Small group process is not only modeled, but it is experienced and retained.

Whatever the situation, there are several essential concepts that build healthy characteristics and unique mindsets to help give the small group experience a strong start. Without much preparation or consideration of group process, the designated time together can become directionless, uninteresting, and less than a desirable experience. For this reason, each chapter presents the essentials of leading in the context of the specific topic of focus. It is not meant to be exhaustive; rather, a means of guidance by presenting the basic essentials for starting well. A suggested reading list for digging deeper and extra resources to enhance understanding are included for further consideration. Since my small group experience is ministering in the context of New England, particular information concerning the sometimes challenging mindset of New Englanders and all it implies, is elaborated.

The following content has been my resource for the one-day training sessions I have presented over the past several years. It reflects the many teachers and authors who have helped shape my philosophy of small group process. It is reinforced with many years of my consistently leading numerous and diverse small groups. And it developed through the input of many colleagues as we shared experiences, creativity, and resources over the years. The material is useful for leadership and group evaluation, for fresh and innovative ideas, and for a deeper understanding of how groups function at their best. Unless stated otherwise, all Scripture noted for the biblical foundation of the material presented and the Bible study for each chapter is the New International Version.

Renewing Your Church Through Healthy Small Groups can be an important leadership training tool. Each chapter includes the biblical basis for the content, story telling, skills and concepts, and implementation suggestions. The chapters conclude with an interactive small group Bible study experience. Meeting for eight weeks during the week at the church or in the home, will provide the *hands on* experience that develops confidence for stepping into the leadership role. The time segments of the small group sessions may vary according to preference, but ideally the group should meet for a minimum of ninety minutes. In order to preserve the quality of the time together, reading the chapter and completing the corresponding Bible study is a prerequisite.

Enjoy the journey! As future small group leaders, be committed to lead with excellence as you strive to build intentional relationships for spiritual renewal. May God bless you as you become more informed, encouraged, and confident while working your way through *Renewing Your Church Through Healthy Small Groups.*

RENEWAL:
BEING AS GOD INTENDED

"Whatever renewal takes place in our lives
flows from our faith-relationship to Christ.
Instead of inheriting guilt, corruption and death
from the first Adam, we now inherit peace,
healing and life from the Messiah."

Richard Lovelace, *Renewal as a Way of Life*

What comes to your mind when you hear the word renewal? Do you think of reminders of dues for a club or organizational membership? Perhaps the term makes you think of a stripping agent, an eye solution, or an urban renovation.

Renewal, according to the dictionary, simply means, to make new or as if new again. Perhaps this is the kind of renewal that the Old Testament prophet Jeremiah was voicing when he wrote: "I will put my law in their minds and write it on their hearts. I will be their God, and they will be my people" (Jeremiah 31:33). Jeremiah certainly seems to be talking about a powerful time of renewal, a returning to what God ultimately planned for His people. In fulfillment of prophecy, we see Jesus giving his life for our salvation, promising a Comforter and Enabler, and experiencing the Holy Spirit making old hearts new. In this sense, renewal suggests returning to and being as God intended.

Renewal always begins with God at work in the life of the individual; and it always involves coming face to face with God's holiness and our own sinfulness. The gospel writer, Matthew, relates Jesus' words as he tells the people about God's kingdom; "Blessed are those who mourn, for they will be comforted" (Matthew 5:4). If we were to see ourselves through God's perspective, we would see how far short we fall from what God intends for us to be. This awakening should cause us to mourn over our condition. We tend, however, to be quite complacent with using our own lens and settling for far less than God has intended, and to that end, mandated. For the person coming to Christ for the first time, or perhaps for the disciple who has become indifferent in his or her faith, repentance becomes a turning point, not only turning from sin, but also turning to God for faith and guidance.

Nehemiah is often used as an example of renewal: the building of community, the restoring of walls, and the renewal of faith foundations. The process began with the recognition of sin and a soul yearning for repentance (Nehemiah 1:5-10). God honored Nehemiah's desire. Repentance expresses the idea of lamenting, grieving, to be sorry for or to change one's mind by turning back or returning to right ways and means. "Doing what was right in their own eyes" became the downfall of the nation of Israel. God sent out prophets with a message of repentance, calling his people towards total change in their attitude concerning sin by turning to righteousness and entering new fellowship with God. Our culture today is extremely self-directed and driven by "doing what is right in our own eyes" as well. We should not ignore this. Christ left us with a mandate to tell people the good news of salvation and to make disciples. We all need to go back to the basics, to God's Word, and to be as God intended. What better venue for people to come face to face with God and with God's truth than authentic spiritual community through a healthy small group!

Renewal starts with repentance. It involves a change of mind regarding a person's sin and not being afraid to call sin "sin." It creates the understanding of an individual's helplessness before a Holy God. It requires that we express regret or sorrow for all that we do that displeases God. It calls us to mourn over our selfish condition. Repentance is at the heart of the message of the gospel of Jesus Christ. Renewal, then, becomes the blessing of repentance, a returning to seek the face of God and do what is right in God's estimation. Paul challenges his readers to "be renewed in the attitude of your minds; and to put on the new self, created to be like God in true righteousness and holiness" (Ephesians 4:23-24). To the Romans he writes: "do not conform any longer to the pattern of this world, but be transformed by the renewing of your mind" (Romans 12:2). When a small group has created a comfortable, healthy spiritual community, people are honored in their spiritual journey, renewal is evident, and by God's grace, life transformation happens!

We observe powerful culture change through reviewing the great awakenings and revivals that God brought forth through Spirit filled people such as John Wesley, George Whitefield, Jonathan Edwards, Charles Finney, Billy Sunday, Billy Graham, and many others. Repentance was preached, lives were changed, and the culture was affected. The rippling effect of the renewals was powerful, building and building with a significant spiritual impact. They all began with the proclamation of God's truth. People came face to face with their sin. Love, care, and discipleship carried new believers into a powerful relationship with God. Lives were transformed. We have remarkable power on which to grasp daily for renewing our lives by knowing and experiencing God... and that can happen in a healthy small group striving for authentic spiritual community.

Renewal is knowing God as He intended us to know Him. It is examining oneself in light of Scripture. It is having a thirst for God such as did King David as he cried out: "O God, you are my God. Earnestly I seek you. My soul thirsts for you, my body longs for you in a dry and weary land where there is no water" (Psalm 63:1). In our dry and weary culture, we see much wickedness. We, in the church, need to provide venues for hearing God's Word in a caring, relational setting, for it is here that disciples are made and encouraged in their spiritual journeys as they follow Jesus. We have a sovereign, transcendent, living God who acts and intervenes in the lives of individuals and healthy small groups can be the perfect place for that to happen.

Sometimes the word renewal is inaccurately associated with the appearance of numerical growth or expanding buildings. It is helpful to consider this misunderstanding by exploring some research. There are many resources available describing the important variables in creating healthy church life.[1] I am

---

1 Stephen A. Macchia, Becoming a Healthy Church: Ten Characteristics (Grand Rapids, Michigan: Baker Books, 1999). Additional resources: Christian A. Schwarz, Natural Church Development: A Guide to Eight Essential Qualities of Healthy Churches (St. Charles,

particularly drawn to one study for various reasons. Rev. Dr. Stephen Macchia, trusted friend, spiritual leader and mentor, at the time of this particular study was president of Vision New England.

This most helpful study involved months of strategic dialogue and discussion with many churches by asking questions such as: "What does a healthy church look like today?[2] Is it one with a strong choir with lots of wealthy executives in the pews? Is it high attendance, an effective Christian Formation offering, or a thriving missions program?" Throughout the study the team identified ten characteristics of a healthy church all stemming from the outgrowth of hundreds of discussions, several years of field-testing, and two major surveys. The resulting ten characteristics include: (1) God's empowering presence; (2) God-exalting worship; (3) spiritual disciplines; (4) learning and growing in community; (5) a commitment to loving and caring relationships; (6) servant-leadership development; (7) an outward focus; (8) wise administration and accountability; (9) networking with the body of Christ; and (10) stewardship and generosity[3]. All of these characteristics reflect healthy small group life, particularly characteristics four (learning and growing in community), five (a commitment to loving and caring relationships), and seven (an outward focus).

Evaluating our church with these ten characteristics in mind helps us to understand areas of weakness and strength and to prayerfully build where needed. If we long for renewal, evaluating our lives as a disciple of Christ and

---

Illinois: Church Smart Resources, 1996); Leith Anderson, A Church for the 21st Century (Minneapolis, MN: Bethany House Publishers, 1992); Bill and Lynne Hybels, Rediscovering Church (Grand Rapids: Zondervan Publishing House, 1995); George Barna, The Habits of Highly Effective Churches (Ventura: Regal Books, 1999).

2   Macchia, "what would you say constitutes the foundation of a healthy church ministry? Many slogans suggest ideas, but wouldn't you agree that the Word of God and prayer are fundamental? They are two of God's greatest gifts to us. In them we discover God through his Spirit. In them we grow in our relationship with our Savior. In them we learn about where we have come from and who we are to become today. Scriptures and prayer, we found, are at the heart of every truly healthy church." 16,18.

3   Ibid.,7. In 1997 during the annual Vision New England Congress Conference, 1,899 attendees from the group of 8,000 took ten minutes to complete a computerized, self-administered survey regarding their attitudes about church. Respondents were queried specifically on their demographics, religiosity, and church involvement. In keeping with the study objectives, respondents also were asked to assess the Ten Characteristics of a Healthy Church. Each of the ten characteristics was grouped into three key elements – an exercise that resulted in thirty attitude statements. Regardless of the race, gender, denomination age, number of years as a believer, or responsibility in the church, the basic rank order of the ten characteristics held constant.

as leaders becomes an important variable in preparing each individual person. If renewal starts with the individual, it will result in a rippling effect pouring out new life, new growth, and life-transforming environments into our churches. And, if renewal happens in community, we can see why characteristics four, five, and seven listed above are to be carefully evaluated and considered within the mission and goals of our church life.

Renewal does not necessarily mean converts, church numerical growth or financial success. It does, however, reflect the quality of spiritual life, the awareness of sin, and the greatness and holiness of God along with His power and authority to forgive and make right. It is within this community of love that each person can be gripped with God's Word and the implication for right living as children of God.

The small group becomes a powerful venue for renewal as we build a caring community through strong relationships. We are not called to grow spiritually in isolation, but to experience and share God's grace with one another. Paul reminds us of God's powerful grace and mercy we have received when he wrote to the church at Ephesus: "And I pray that you, being rooted and established in love, may have power, together with all the saints, to grasp how wide and long and high and deep is the love of Christ, and to know this love that surpasses knowledge – that you may be filled to the measure of all the fullness of God" (Ephesians 3:16-19). Renewal begins when God opens ears, eyes, and minds. We become filled with His fullness.

When there is repentance, a striving to know God and His power, lives are changed. Renewal happens and God brings people new hearts, new attitudes, new mindsets, and new gifts. Hope becomes the anchor of the soul for standing firm during difficult times and in a difficult culture. Statistics show that healthy growing churches are ones with healthy small groups.[4] It becomes essential to be intentional about forming these groups where people build meaningful relationships with one another and especially with God through Jesus Christ and in the power of the Holy Spirit.

The Holy Spirit brings renewal to open minds and willing hearts. Just think of the potential huge impact on your church when authentic spiritual community is flourishing within small groups, when they multiply and envelop the church

---

4   Ibid., Chapters 4 & 5; Schwarz, Characteristic #6: Holistic Small Groups, 32.

body, and when the gospel reaches out to those in the town and surrounding areas. Concerning church growth, spiritual and numerical, Christian Schwarz remarked, "If we were to identify any one principle as the 'most important,' then without a doubt it would be the multiplication of small groups."[5] The church is and continues to be renewed through healthy small groups!

HINDRANCES

There are, however, impediments that hinder the formation of effective and thriving small groups. These impediments can be simply a lack of healthy small group process or as often encountered here in New England, prevailing mindsets that either prevent people from wanting to join a small group or limit the freedom of their group interaction... if they take the risk to join. We need to take a look at what they are and their implications for ministry.

One barrier to forming healthy small groups is simple unawareness of what a small group can be and do in the lives of interested people. It is for this reason that the following chapters attempt to inform and encourage future leaders, or remind current leaders, of concepts, skills, and the necessary thoughtful development of the particular leadership commitment they have made.

Here in New England there are additional barriers involving particular traits that have developed since New England was founded. These barriers are necessary to understand as we design and implement a healthy small group. A strategic study focusing on the New England mindset was researched through a partnership with Vision New England and The Ockenga Institute at Gordon-Conwell Theological Seminary. Data was collected from a wide variety of sources: nationwide social surveys, the U.S. Census Bureau, and other demographic sources, polling organizations, marketing studies, economic and business organizations, personal interviews, and books. The Advisory Committee critiqued the data. Each individual on the committee was assigned one particular trait to further explore and present as a research project. From this research, the resulting eight unique characteristics of the New England mindset was presented through area seminars to interested churches throughout the New England area.[6]

---

5   Schwarz, 32.

6   New England Research Project, What Are The Unique Traits of New Englanders? A preliminary study of New England Culture, Gordon-Conwell Theological Seminary, South Hamilton, MA, 1995. For more information please contact The Ockenga Institute at

Being a New Englander (and in the minds of New Englanders, that means at least three generations have lived in New England!), I am aware of our unique and often obstinate behavior. New England draws many people to the city areas by being on the leading edge of development in business, finance, technology, medicine, the fine arts, and higher education. Churches flourish with diverse backgrounds and experiences. The suburban church, however, often reflects a totally different mindset, making ministry through the larger New England area a great paradox.

As I attend various conferences with colleagues from different parts of the United States and hear some of the creative ideas and procedures, it never ceases to amaze me how so many people elsewhere seem to be easily drawn into small group ministry. It seems to be more difficult here in New England, but God is at work! Implementation, however, continues to be a challenging experience. Take a look at these eight unique characteristics. For your benefit, I have included implications for small group process to each trait. If you are not from New England, you may find that they reflect the mindset of your culture as well. However, New Englanders, in exhibiting these eight traits, do so with extra vigor and determination!

NEW ENGLANDERS TEND TO:

1. **Resist change**: Despite the pervasiveness of modern media and technology, old attitudes and behavior persist in many arenas of life in New England. A familiar comment, "but we've always done it this way," can frustrate ministry leaders when considering new options. However, once New Englanders buy into the new concept, they tend to be faithfully committed.
2. **Value tradition**: Tradition permeates all facets of life in New England. New Englanders tend to have a sense of continuity with the past, partially because the past is so rich with significant events. There are many areas of life where this emphasis on tradition reveals itself and creates barriers for cutting edge ministry. It is important to be balanced with new ministry offerings.
3. **Be Roman Catholic**: While Roman Catholic loyalties tend to run deeper in ethnic groups, the number of Roman Catholics hovers around 60 percent of New Englanders and churches need to consider this statistic in

planning ministry. Often there is little background in Bible study or experience for reading and understanding Scripture without the authority figure. This opens many opportunities for forming discipleship groups for learning the basics.

4. **Have a secular mindset**: Despite the fact that many of New England's best-known educational institutions were founded by churches, the secular mindset became dominant at most of these institutions of learning many decades ago, with the students carrying that mindset into daily life. In the Boston area there are over forty-three universities or higher education institutions. At the same time, Boston is one of the lowest cities in the country with interest in reading the Bible.[7] Healthy small groups can create the interest and develop disciples for Christ.

5. **Be self-reliant**: In the northern parts of New England, rugged winters tend to isolate people and force them to become self-reliant. Individuals and families also generate much of the economic activity. Often this reflects in being reluctant to form teams, to completely depend on others, or to expose a personal need one might have. New Englanders tend not to rely on prayer.

6. **Be reserved**: Being cautious with new ideas and developing relationships, New Englanders are often perceived as unfriendly, but are in most cases merely cautious. Achieving the level of intimacy and trust is harder for New Englanders once they commit to a small group. Leaders need to hurry slowly with risk taking ideas for interaction. Self-disclosure is often hampered by the more natural response that personal life is private.

7. **Favor insiders**: New Englanders are often considered distrustful of any influences that might change their way of life. This includes new people coming into the community with new ideas! Many churches have the mindset that, if truth were to be known, they do not want to grow. It means change and unfamiliarity. In fact, someone new might sit in his or her self-claimed pew. This attitude often affects their passion for outreach and evangelism.

---

7 The Barna Group, "New Research Exploring Faith in America's Largest Markets Produces Surprises" (Ventura: CA, August 23, 2005). Sunday school attendance among adults is most common in Salt Lake City, and least common in Portland, Maine. Involvement in an adult small group is most prolific in Shreveport, Louisiana. The three markets with the lowest rates of small group participation are Albany (NY), Boston (MA), and Providence (RI). Believing that God is "the all-knowing, all-powerful creator of the universe who still rules it today" is most common in Tulsa. It is least predominant in Boston and San Francisco. One out of every six residents of Massachusetts, Connecticut, and Washington are atheist or agnostic -- nearly double the national average.

8. **Operate locally:** With a high value of tradition and a tendency to prefer insiders, it is not surprising to find that local control is favored over state and federal governments. This mindset is often demonstrated through being insular rather than interacting with or forming ministry teams with other churches in the area.

ADDITIONAL HINDRANCES

Transition: Many New England urban areas tend to be very transitional. This trend is also somewhat evident across the country. People come and go very quickly; making it difficult to create lasting relationships or long-term leadership commitments. When people know they are in an area for a short period of time, there seems to be less motivation to take opportunities for creating meaningful relationships. The younger generation tends not to fall into this category of behavior as much as middle age, but for me as minister of small groups at my city church, fifty percent of the congregation transitioned in less than two years! Now there's a challenge for training leaders and investing in their lives. However, through this experience, it became an exciting opportunity to equip, mentor, and send away with the dream of expanding the vision for healthy small groups somewhere else in the world.

Busyness: Life for everyone seems overwhelmingly busy. People spend longer hours at work, experience increasing family demands and commitments, and exclaim that they are just too busy to join a small group. When in the week is it possible to set aside time to meet with a small group of people? Those of us who manage small group ministries hear these comments continually. In casting a vision for small groups and for leading small groups, there must be a sense of spiritual need and excellence in the ministry for people to realize that the experience is worth being a priority in their busy schedule.

Ministry demands: Within the church setting we keep the church calendar filled with options and required committee meetings. It is quite understandable when a person has two or three meetings a week that he or she does not want to be out one more night. It is here that turning a committee into a community is a valuable option.[8] Creating a caring community while focusing on a task within the life of the church is very workable and satisfying.

---

8   Roberta Hestenes, Turning Committees into Communities (Colorado Springs: NavPress, 1991) is an excellent pamphlet for assisting the vision for designing present committees to function more strategically as caring communities.

These are important demographic issues to understand as we consider our ministries. If a church has never had small groups, this is change. "We have never done that before" becomes a strong reason for not venturing into new methods for creating community. Tradition is important, implying that things should be done the way they have been done for the last two hundred years. If we are reserved and people shy away from self-disclosure, it is hard to create meaningful, vulnerable, truth-telling, trusting environments. If we favor insiders, then we have to agree that we are not focused on church growth. Besides, bringing new people into the church creates change and challenges the comfort zone. If we do not plan to be in one location very long, if we are too busy in other areas of our lives, or if the ministry in church life for which we have volunteered or been elected gives us reasons for not becoming involved in small groups, the small group ministry leaders need to pursue more creative thinking for viable options in providing caring environments for the church family. Building caring, trusting environments for growing spiritually with God and one another is not a church program; it is an important lifestyle commitment as a believer. If we yearn for personal renewal and church renewal, the healthy small group is a perfect environment!

Knowing your people, the church culture and the culture of your area becomes imperative before beginning small groups. It means you hurry slowly, especially here in New England, and do your homework in order for people to be willing to take a risk and buy into new ideas and venues, or consider joining the ones in place. These traits and hindrances become important to understand before ministry is designed or carefully considered when evaluating and making changes. And in time, our goal for renewal begins to materialize, God is glorified, and we reap the rewards through hearing people tell their stories about their life-changing experience in a healthy small group. God has set the scene for a rippling effect.

For example, early in the formation of the small group ministry at my city church, I interviewed two people from different small groups during the "ministry moment" segment of the service. (Testimony concerning personal experience in a small group before the church congregation is powerful advertising) The age difference was intentional. On my right was an eighteen-year-old young man who enthusiastically talked specifically about the changes God had made in his life through his belonging to an awesome small group. On my left was an eighty-one year old woman who, with great enthusiasm, explained that she had never experienced a small group until this particular time in her life. She elaborated on how the various one another mandates of Scripture had come alive to her, how close and significant relationships had developed with peers and the few young people included in the group, and how thrilled she was that God had given her this life-changing experience so late in life!

Renewal. Scripture supports and experience confirms that God renews hearts and minds through a small, but significant, authentic Christian community of people. It is here where His people gather in His name, strive to become godly and learn to listen to His voice. God called the prophet Isaiah for His prophetic purpose in giving a message to Israel: "listen, listen, hear and awake" are repeated words throughout Isaiah chapter 51. He challenged them to remember and understand what God had done for "but one." It was a message of hope and encouragement. The message continues to have huge implications for us today. We need to consider our faith-relationship with God through Jesus Christ, the empowering presence of the Holy Spirit, and expect renewal to transcend our spiritual communities and church life.

GETTING TO KNOW YOU

1. TELL

Take some time to get acquainted as you begin this training journey together. Asking safe, simple questions begins the process of telling life stories and getting to know one another. Use the questions below or ask something fun that comes to mind!

- » Where were you born?
- » Where did you live when you were 12 and what did you like about that location?
- » If you had a free day this week, how would you spend your time?
- » If you were being shipped to a remote island and could bring one favorite thing, what would that item be? Why?

2. DISCUSS

To pray for and anticipate renewal in your church and community is powerful. Begin your time together by talking about renewal and the implications for your church family. Identify a few barriers for creating healthy small groups that come to mind from the chapter contents. What will be your first steps to thinking strategically in overcoming those barriers?

FINDING GOD

Read Matthew 6:33

3. SCRIPTURE

We all have spiritual journeys. At times they are seeking God and yearning for His presence. Yet, there are periods when we seem to be running away from His love and influence. God prompts us to seek Him, and when we do, we find Him! Take a few minutes to briefly describe your experience. Consider your time carefully. Remember, if there are ten of you and you each try to take ten minutes, you won't have time to hear from everyone. There will be many opportunities to share your Christian experiences more deeply as you travel together through this training. Here are some questions you might consider responding to briefly:

> » If you were raised in a Christian home, do you remember the defining moment when your parents' faith became your faith? When and where?
> » If you were not raised in a Christian home, when and how did you first hear about and respond to the good news of Jesus Christ? In what way did this news affect your life?
> » What motivates you to be part of the small group ministry? What would you like to see God do in and through your group?

4. PRAYER

Pray for one another for the coming week. Pray for your future small group. Pray for personal renewal and church renewal through healthy small groups.

5. PREPARATION

If we pray for and anticipate renewal, the Bible and church history offers powerful examples of just what that might look like. Authentic Christian community is the context for our knowing God, understanding His Word, and the expectations of becoming His children. Significant biblical Community and examples from church history will be explored in the next chapter. In preparing for your next time together, confirm a person who will take on the role of the small group discussion leader. Enjoy reading about biblical community and prepare the Bible study for your group interaction.

"Therefore, I urge you brothers, in view of God's mercy, to offer your bodies as living sacrifices, holy and pleasing to God—this is your spiritual act of worship. Do not conform any longer to the pattern of this world, but be transformed by the renewing of your mind. Then you will be able to test and approve what God's will is—his good, pleasing and perfect will."

Romans 12:1-2

CHAPTER 2

COMMUNITY: LIFE TOGETHER

"We have one another only through Christ but through Christ, we do have one another wholly and for eternity."

Dietrich Bonhoeffer, *Life Together*

Think of a time when you were deeply encouraged by a group of people. In what way did that experience influence that stage of your life? What happened to create a sense of belonging for you?

God changed the direction of my life through a healthy small group community. I became a believer in my early 20s and during the next few years had several opportunities to be involved with small groups. For various reasons, many of which I will discuss later, I found these groups intimidating, a waste of time, or basically not where I wanted to be. Then one day a friend invited me to a large women's Bible study in which the small group was a vital part. I trusted her endorsement and signed up. It was an intriguing, fun loving, spiritually challenging, and caring group. It wasn't so bad after all! We women learned, laughed, grieved, cared for and held one another accountable while reaching out to those in need through this amazing time together. It caused

me to re-examine my attitude towards small groups while God took me hand-in-hand along an exciting spiritual journey.

When I first committed my time to learning all I could about small group process and the implications for not only the individual, but the church as a whole, the comment I often heard was "Oh, this is a passing fad. It's the buzz word for the moment, but soon it will all pass." But then, with a bit of reflection on the Scriptures, church history, and most certainly the dynamic model Jesus gives us, we soon realize that the small group has been the basis for changing lives for centuries and it is certainly here to stay. It is the small group community where healthy relationships grow, where life stories are shared, and where spiritual growth influences the journey through future life experiences. Small group community is the heart and core for becoming the people of God.

BIBLICAL SNAPSHOTS OF SMALL GROUP COMMUNITY

Observing the biblical examples of life together in small groups paints a picture of God's character and existence. Let's consider a few situations where it is clear that God has ordained a small group of His people to gather for His perfect purpose: (1) the Trinity, (2) Noah, (3) Moses, (4) Daniel, and (5) Jesus.

I. TRINITY

From the very beginning of creation, God has existed in triune community. Although the Trinity is not explicitly stated in the Bible, it is implied throughout all Scripture. For example, (Genesis 1:1-2, 26; Luke 1:35-37; John 14:16-26; John 17; Revelation 1:4-6).[9] We vividly observe the action between the three persons of God: God the Father, the One who sustains and from whom we derive our purpose; God the Son, the One and Only Redeemer of mankind; and God the Holy Spirit, the One who enlightens, comforts, and sanctifies. The three persons of one Holy God entwined throughout creation and the fall and at the very heart of the plan of redemption through Jesus' victory over death. A triune God, the oneness of Deity and the plurality of Persons, interdependent

---

9   We tend to separate the works of God the Father, God the Son, and God the Holy Spirit. A powerful small group study is to trace the Trinity, the works and promises and relationship, through the Old Testament and the New Testament where the three persons of God are working together. The doctrine of the Trinity has value for life and practice. May we give equal love, reverence, and obedience to all three Persons of God.

relationships, offers the hope we have today. God's Word is a timeless truth. As we come together in our small groups, we should strive to know the love of God the Father, the heartbeat of Jesus, God in the flesh, and the power of God's enabling Spirit. We should yearn to be imitators of God longing for life-transformation through spiritual renewal.

2. NOAH

Think about Noah and his group of seven. The Lord grieved over the wickedness on the earth and His heart was filled with pain (Genesis 6:5-6). But Noah was a righteous man, blameless among the people of his time and he walked with God (Genesis 6:9). Noah and his three sons found favor with the Lord and our mighty loving God chose these men and their wives to renew His creation. They existed in cramped quarters with numerous animals, bringing their unique characteristics and environments, and waiting for the moment God would release them from the high waters to the drying soil. (I would imagine there was cause for conflict management skills).

Popular songs and verses most often paint the picture of forty agonizing rainy days within the confines of this dwelling with a few carefully selected two by twos. Upon careful study, one realizes that in fact it was about a year and four months and more animals than examples of wood ark masterpieces would suggest. Nevertheless, this was a chosen community, a small group, strategically placed on the earth for God's perfect purposes; a community that would lead to the rise of God's people.

3. MOSES

God uses community to speak for Him as agents of wisdom. Upon observing Moses' leadership demands, Jethro, Moses' father-in-law, advised Moses that he was not indispensable and could not continue with the responsibilities he had undertaken alone or he would be of no help to anyone (Exodus 18:21-26). As a result of Jethro's concern and on his wise advice, Moses selected and trained God-fearing capable leaders and appointed them over groups of thousands, hundreds, fifties, and tens. The "Jethro" principle has been effectively passed down over generations for delegating responsibilities. Community was formed and honored.

4. DANIEL

In 605 B.C. the young teenager Daniel, along with several other young strapping Jewish men, were victims of the first exile. Transported to a pagan Babylon, Daniel and his three friends, Hananiah, Mishael, and Azariah (later named Shadrach, Meshach, and Abednego) appear to have become what we would consider a small group for encouragement and accountability (Daniel 1:17, 2:17-18). In time, all held prominent positions within the Babylonian government.

As we study their lives in the Book of Daniel, we can surmise that these bonded friends stayed close together helping one another through difficult life experiences. They experienced a trusted, Spirit enabled community of four that honored God for more than seventy years. Challenged with dietary habits, the allegiance to and time for designated moments of prayer, it is evident that God honored their witness and faithfulness throughout the years. This healthy small group of friends, obviously committed to one another, never wavered from their belief and behavior in the profound truth that God is sovereign. They were significantly blessed. How difficult, if not impossible, it would have been to survive alone.

5. JESUS

The example we see modeled by Jesus in the New Testament has become the inspiration for small group ministry throughout history. Jesus selected this diverse small group of twelve men whom he trained to one day take over his ministry and begin to spread Christianity throughout the world (Mark 3:13-19). Their basic training was built around an accountability group where they learned by watching Jesus as an example. They shared in leadership responsibilities with on the job training and were evaluated through reporting back in debriefing opportunities (Mark 6:7, 30). At times they appeared to be slow learners. Isn't it easy to read of their lack of understanding, their doubts, their we don't get it responses and wonder why it was so hard for Jesus to get through to them? I question if we would have behaved any differently! God uses the interactions with Jesus and his disciples as a model from which leaders gain powerful insight in forming authentic Christian community.

Fear and doubt entered the lives of Jesus' disciples during his trial, death, and resurrection. Times got tough and they scattered. Sending the message of denial and failure to the crowds, they misunderstood his kingdom and doubted his resurrected appearance. But Jesus, with his eternal love, gathered his "walking wounded" in an upper room and helped them to come to grips with their responses. They learned to trust, forgive, encourage, and support one another as Jesus ministered to them and the Holy Spirit sustained them over the next fifty days. He encouraged them with the promise of his comfort and power in the coming Spirit (John 20:21, 30). Their faith, hope and trust were renewed.

Talk about renewal! After the coming of the Holy Spirit at Pentecost, the motley small group was transformed. As the gospel was proclaimed and Scripture states, on that day three thousand experienced life-transformation as they committed to the Christian faith. Acts 2:42-47; 4:32-37 is most descriptive of the confident believers as they devoted themselves to the apostles' teaching and to the fellowship, to the breaking of bread, to prayer, and the sharing of necessary goods for those in need as they met in the temple courts and in homes.

COMMUNITY EXAMPLES THROUGH PASSAGE OF TIME

Through the passing of time, we see strong examples of small group renewal. Consider the Reformation of the sixteenth century. Spearheaded in Germany by Martin Luther (1483-1546), but supported by many others, the reformers sought renewal and change within the church. Through the revitalization of God's Word, the reformers confronted the existing church and its strong focus on papal and sacramental authority and human tradition. "Scripture Alone" for justification was a severe contradiction to the existing church and its teaching. Luther's vision was to bring the truth of Scripture to the common person. Grace was God's gift to those who placed their faith in the saving work of Jesus Christ; with no strings attached. Rather than seeing reformation within the church, Luther was excommunicated. Here began the powerful Protestant movement.

Philip Schaff, the famous church historian, states that the Reformation "marked the gradual transition from the Middle Ages to modern times, from the universal acceptance of the papal theocracy in Western Europe to the assertion of national independence, from the supreme authority of the priesthood to the intellectual and spiritual freedom of the individual."[10] One of the central goals of the Reformation was to bring the Scriptures to the common person,

---

10 Phillip Schaff, History of the Christian Church (Grand Rapids, Michigan: Eerdmans, reprint 1984, Vol. vi), 1.

the "priesthood of believers." First and foremost were laity small groups who met for prayer and the study of Scripture. Scripture was read with a new sense of anticipation of what might be possible as a consequence of acting in faith. For Martin Luther, faith was to be nourished and strengthened through reflection and meditation on Scripture. For this reason, small groups were formed to help people integrate their belief and behavior, their faith and their work.

John Calvin (1509-1564), the French Reformer who ultimately spent most of his preaching, teaching and writing years in Switzerland, attempted to evangelize his native France through the venue of small groups. These were strategic small groups of laity who met regularly for prayer and the study of Scripture.[11] Although considered a bit more radical, Calvin supported the Reformed focus of "Scripture Alone" for justification. His contribution Institutes of the Christian Religion was one of the most important writings of the sixteenth century. Calvin claimed his reason for writing this work was to allow his readers to have easy access to the Word of God and to progress in it without stumbling.[12]

Alister M\^cGrath, world recognized British theologian, conveys not only the Reformers concerns, but ours today in saying "being deeply immersed in the world, Christians are at risk of losing their distinctiveness, morale, and vitality. The community of faith provides a vital network of support and nourishment for those committed to the world."[13]

John Wesley (1703-1791) was the most famous leader and creator of the Evangelical movement in England. John and his brother Charles formed a small group to aid one another in their studies, to read helpful books, and to participate in frequent communion. This was known as the Holy Club.[14] And for its disciplined ways, it was given the name Methodist. With the huge impact on the lives of the group, this small group format was eventually to become the strategic plan for spiritual growth within the Wesleyan movement.

At the heart of John Wesley's discipleship and renewal system was "the class meetings." The class meetings proved to be an excellent environment

---

11 Alister M\^cGrath, Spirituality in an Age of Change (Grand Rapids, Michigan: Zondervan, 1994), 54.

12 Ibid., 55.

13 Ibid., 114.

14 Kenneth Scott Latourette, A History of Christianity: Reformation to the Present (San Francisco: Harper, 1975), 1023.

for life transformation and became a pivotal element of the Methodist movement, blending belief and behavior for the integrity of their faith. The class meeting challenged the small group with the key principles of New Testament Christianity: personal growth, accountability, and spiritual stewardship by "bearing one another's burdens" and "speaking the truth in love."[15] Wesley made sure every believer was engaged in a small group, and through this powerful movement, the English society was largely transformed. So long as it prospered, the class meeting was the institution that did the most to guarantee that church membership was not merely a nominal affiliation.[16]

Puritanism was a movement of the Bible among an increasingly literate people, and an essential accompaniment of its expansion was the publishing of popular versions of the Bible. The earliest of these was the Geneva Version of 1560, with its highly provocative yet immensely instructive marginal notes.[17] Important to the theological education and the commitment to spiritual growth, the Puritans, English and American, called their small groups "private meetings." They were most effective for developing an individual's spirituality.

Meeting at least weekly, there were several reasons for these gatherings: (1) in such a small group, Christians could more easily express "love for one another;" (2) as a community of prayer it could exercise "earnest prayer for the Church" of which it was a part; (3) by "timely exhortation" members could apply the Gospel to others in a direct way; (4) it gave members the opportunity to engage in "instructing and teaching one another; as occasion serves;" (5) it could be a means of God's grace "in comforting those that be sad" or in mourning; (6) it was a forum in which members, even those "fallen with a spirit of meekness," could learn to express their faith and the gifts of the Spirit more boldly. These were the churches' goals in promoting private meetings among their membership through out the century.[18]

Puritanism would become one of the most vital elements in the foundations of American thought and culture. Throughout the years, small groups

---

15 Michael D. Henderson, John Wesley's Class Meetings (Nappanee, Indiana: Francis Asbury Press, 1997), 14.

16 Sydney E. Ahlstrom, A Religious History of the American People (New Haven and London: Yale University Press, 1972), 373.

17 Ibid., 92.

18 Charles E.Hambrick-Stowe, The Practice of Piety (Chapel Hill, North Carolina: University of North Carolina Press, 1982), 138.

have been powerfully used by God to lay the foundation for spiritual growth, renewal, and great awakenings. It is our model today for small groups designed for growing into authentic Christian community.

God intended us to be in relationship with Him and with others. There is a large unfilled hole in our soul when that is neglected or prevented. Being in relationship with God and His creation is the heartbeat of the Christian life and it is the means for allowing the Holy Spirit to change us into His image. Authentic Christian community is the relational environment for this life change and what better model could we design than a small group of people devoted to growing spiritually and seeking the will of God!

ACKNOWLEDGING THE "ONE ANOTHERS"

In reading the New Testament, God opens our eyes to see a plethora of "one anothers" clearly expressing what we as believers need to hear and act upon. We are to: "love one another, be devoted to one another, honor one another, accept one another, serve one another, be kind and compassionate to one another, forgive one another, submit to one another, do not lie to one another, teach and admonish one another, encourage one another, build up one another, live in peace with one another, spur one another along, confess your sins to one another, pray for one another, have fellowship with one another," just to list a few. How necessary a reflective, responsive community becomes in our daily lives. Healthy community is a taste of what is to come for us in eternity.

COMMUNITY AND ALL IT IMPLIES

Community is an interesting word and loaded with all kinds of nuances. Several years ago I was at a dinner preceding a conference where Bill Hybels, Pastor of the Willow Creek Church, was the keynote speaker. He prepared us for his message by requesting that we, during our meal, develop a definition of community. As we energetically tied descriptive words together to complete our task, we were delighted to hear the simple, but powerful words he had chosen to define the essence of community: "to love and be loved, to know and be known, to serve and be served, and to celebrate and be celebrated."

Bill Donahue and Russ Robinson have written about several issues within the life of a small group that give rise to tension. These authors added a necessary ingredient to the original definition noted above: "to admonish and to be admonished."[19] Scripture addresses this issue in several references, and certainly is clear in 2 Timothy 3:16-17: "All Scripture is God-breathed and is useful for teaching, rebuking, correcting and training in righteousness, so that the man of God may be thoroughly equipped for every good work." Admonishing, at the right time and in the right manner is an essential part of the package.

Henri Nouwen,[20] the late writer and Christian thinker, who challenged us all to deepen our intimacy with Christ, emphasized a shepherding small group as one comprised of people who "know and are known, who care and are cared for, who forgive and are being forgiven, who love and are being loved.[21] Throughout our time together we will be revisiting these various attributes of small group community. First, let's take a closer look at knowing, loving, serving, admonishing, and celebrating and what they imply in the life of a healthy small group striving for personal and church renewal.

I. KNOW

"A man of many companions may come to ruin,
but there is a friend who sticks closer than a brother."

Proverbs 18:24

Knowing one another becomes far deeper than, "Yes, I know her." We often know about others, but not their heart and soul. In a biblical sense, knowing includes the dynamic of experiencing their existence in an intimate spiritual relationship, becoming close brothers and sisters in Christ. It becomes far more significant than just knowing about one another. Unfortunately many of our small groups do not travel around the bases of life with healthy group process and therefore remain at a superficial level of knowledge.

---

19 Bill Donahue and Russ Robinson, Walking the Small Group Tightrope (Grand Rapids: Zondervan , 2003), 74-75. This is an excellent resource for understanding and dealing with the tensions every small group experiences in the process of reaching authentic spiritual community.

20 Henri Nouwen (1932-1996), pastor and writer was spiritual director of L'Arche Daybreak in Toronto, Canada, a community where men and women with disabilities and their assistants create a home for one another.

21 Henri Nouwen, In The Name of Jesus (New York, New York: Crossroads, 1994), 43.

The getting to know you process starts with friendship and self-disclosure. Gradually not only do we become more familiar with one another, but certainly with God and therefore with ourselves in a more honest assessment in light of God's Word. Knowing God allows the life transformation to happen. This takes intentional leadership and later chapters will explain creative ways of achieving this goal.

2. LOVE

> "A new command I give you: Love one another.
> As I have loved you, you must love one another.
> Then others will know that you are my disciples,
> if you love one another."
>
> *John 13:34*

As we think about self-disclosure as the key for getting to know someone, we may or may not relate, feel comfortable with, or feel attracted to everyone in our group. That is not the issue. Christ has given us a mandate to love with love that only he can provide through the Holy Spirit. We are all recipients of God's grace and mercy. Therefore, we honor each other and strive to love with God's love. Think about times that God has allowed you to love someone whom you never would in your own strength. (And of course there are those people who have prayed equally hard to love you!) Peter tells us to "love deeply" (1 Peter 4:8) and if we have the Holy Spirit in us, he will enable us to do just that. It takes willingness and humility to look through the lens of Christ, which is love. We love because he first loved us and God has put us together in a small group spiritual community.

3. SERVE

> "Let us not love with words or tongue
> but with actions and in truth."
>
> *1 John 3:18*

Prior to Jesus giving the new command, (John 13:34-35), he had demonstrated his love to his motley group by being a humble servant-leader. Jesus, God in the flesh, knows and loves each of them. Stooping and washing twenty-four dirty, grimy feet, two of which would run off into the night in betrayal, Jesus demonstrates his great love for them in serving in a humble unexpected task. We don't often wash one another's feet in a small group setting, but reality tells us that at some point, someone will be in need and benefit from the mutual support of their small group. It may not come as a trumpet sound, but a sensitive, caring, supportive small group that gets to know and love deeply one another with God's love will intuitively know when someone is in need. And, that need requires action. As people serve and are served, within the group, church or community, a gracious environment is created.

4. ADMONISH

> "Correct, rebuke and encourage
> with great patience and careful instruction."

2 Timothy 4:2

Does striving for the "love deeply" mean we only affirm what is good in people and never confront sin? Unfortunately, many groups never reach that trusting stage of effectiveness in the group life. Facing personal and corporate sin and pain is part of the spiritual journey. Larry Crabb states, "A connecting community, where each member is joined together in dynamic spiritual union, is a healing community."[22] Getting to know and love each other is valued and, in time, admonishment is earned. "Speaking the truth in love, we will in all things grow up into him who is the head, that is, Christ" (Ephesians 4:15) strongly urges us to admonish in love and with the gentleness of God's grace. This process will be covered more thoroughly in our chapter on conflict management.

---

22 Larry Crabb, The Safest Place on Earth (Nashville, Tennessee: Word Publishing, 1999), 8. Larry Crabb, a licensed psychotherapist, and founder of New Way Ministries, has written many significant books on counseling, connecting, spiritual community and helpful tools for understanding ourselves, others and most importantly where God should fit into the picture.

5. CELEBRATE

"Celebrate that your name is written in heaven."

Luke 10:20

Every small group should take time to celebrate their life together. We are God's children and heirs of His heavenly kingdom. We have the power of his Spirit in us and working through us, regardless of our diversity, personal attraction, or position in life. Believe that God has formed your group for a reason. Celebrate and honor one another. Celebrate what God is doing in and through your group. Celebrate God's presence in difficult and joyful times throughout your shared journey. Celebrate the gifts God has given each of you as you get to know, love, and serve one another.

So, you see, there's community where everyone may know your name, but not the real you, and there's authentic spiritual community where truth and life intersect, where people care about your life issues and support and encourage you in your responses. It moves knowledge and love from the head to the heart, deep into your soul and springs forth as life-transformation. That is being open and honest before God and one another and ultimately living to glorify God.

THE CHANGING CULTURE

In our changing culture and day-to-day challenges, our lives often are frantic with deadlines, questionable priorities and overly tight schedules. We tend to be human doers and not human beings and we are in danger of losing our meaningful connections and the desire to spend quality time developing relationships where we can model Christian love and care for one another. Cultivating our souls with spiritual nourishment is a necessary discipline. Isaiah 30:15a is our challenge: "In repentance and rest is your salvation, in quietness and trust is your strength." We would do well to heed these words as we gather to encourage one another on our spiritual journeys.

Unless we make wise decisions about how we spend our time and what will be our priorities, today's busy culture hardly allows us moments for rest and quietness. Culture has changed dramatically in the span of my life. When I was young, things were different. My parents moved our family while I was spending time with my grandmother in Maine. My first morning in my new home was full of adventure. Our street was less than a mile with houses evenly spaced, but not too close. I managed to find someone home at each house as I knocked and asked, "Does anyone my age live here?" I was 6 years old. I found one girl and four boys who would attend and graduate with me from the same school eleven years later.

Many years have passed but I continue to remember most of the neighborhood: the frail schoolteacher, the hyper dentist, the elderly church choir director, the humorous hardware store owner, and the mothers and fathers of my friends. Not only did we know who they were and what they did, but took notice when the sad times hit, as well as the greatly anticipated celebrations.

Until field hockey and basketball years began in Junior High, my sisters and I came home from school to homemade cookies and an afternoon of creative activity. No, there was no television during the day back then! I rode my bike for miles without parental worry; we often left the front door of our home unlocked when we went out and the keys in the car while we shopped. Was my life unusual? No, that's how life was back then. We had community ... a safe community in the home and neighborhood. We had a sense of belonging and connection with those who lived around us. I enjoyed my neighbors and they enriched my life.

Looking back further at the turn of the twentieth century, family life was built around the home, the extended family living and working within the home for food and provisions. Each person had a contribution to make and they knew they were important. As life became more urban, the father began his travels to "other places" to earn a living. The shift caused dramatic changes within the continuity of family life as it once was experienced. Yet initially, the mother continued to make her priority the care of her children and of the home.

As time marched on, the shift from these larger family units was reduced to the father, mother, and 2.2 kids, many of whom became "latch key" children while both parents pursued careers. In many cases, the home became the brief stopping point, fast paced, stressful lives developed and one would have to ask, "what happened to the casual meal around the family table?" The age of microwaves and fast food restaurants took over the home baked goodies and the warmth of love.

Where is community in all this? Where do we connect? Who really knows who we are and with what we are struggling? How do we discern that under the smiling face lies a broken, disappointed husband, wife, single adult, or young person? Where's the outlet for intentional face-to-face meetings when one can ask, "How was your day?" and have time to care about the answer?

Having said all this, many families still consist of caring communities. However, the number is staggering of families who do not and are considered dysfunctional. What used to be life together as a loving, caring, supportive home and community has become life alone. Our culture has become fragmented. People need connection. Meaningful relationships, the most necessary component of life, are difficult to find. The era of two working parents continues with constantly increasing number of women who work outside the home. Two families out of three in an average school setting represent divorced parents, single parents, or blended families. The valued role model is hard to find. The neighborhood has broken down where there is less caring, fences go up, alarm systems are installed, and each cries for private, independent, individualized lives. Caring communities in the neighborhood have become the exception to the rule. The fragmented and disconnected lives of our environment therefore demand a place where people feel they are safe and where they belong. A healthy small group can provide that environment for knowing, loving, serving, admonishing, and celebrating. It is the model the early church experienced. The numbers of people coming to faith steadily increased and God's faithfulness in providing for his newly emerging church was evident.

As the younger generation is demonstrating, there's a longing for roots, stability, connection and a quest to experience to some sort of spiritual significance in their lives.[23] One of the main barriers, however, is that many people do not stay in the same place long enough to develop meaningful relationships. Transient connections are easily lost. There seems to be a window of time at the moment where many young people are in search of spiritual truths. For

---

23 Gary L. McIntosh, One Church Four Generations (Grand Rapids: Baker Books, 2002). McIntosh presents the four major generations attending churches today. It is a valuable resource for understanding the mindsets and cultures when developing small group ministries or for small group leaders who make efforts to better understand those in their groups. Additional helps include: Fran Sciacca Generation at Risk (Chicago: Moody Press, 1991); Lewis A. Drummond,. Reaching Generation Next (Grand Rapids: Baker Books, 2002); David W. Henderson, Culture Shift (Grand Rapids: Baker Books, 1998); Gene Edward Veith, Jr., Postmodern Times (Wheaton, Illinois: Crossway Books, 1994). This is an excellent resource for particulars and implications of Postmodern thought and action.

this reason, it is crucial for the Christian church to provide a safe place with listening ears, caring eyes, meaningful relationships and a reason for hope in a chaotic world. A healthy small group can provide the environment for belonging. Small group leaders, committed and equipped with the appropriate skills and vision for creating healthy small groups, can become the most strategic people in the church. Life- transformation happens in small groups.

WHAT SMALL GROUPS SHOULD BE

"A Christian small group is a face-to-face gathering of three to twelve people who commit to coming together on a regular basis for a particular purpose in order to honor God, grow spiritually, connect with fellow believers, and reach out to those in need."

Are small groups an answer to the questions raised by our cultural change? If so, how does one define a small group? Many people unfamiliar with the small group movement, who take an interest in the details of my work and commitment to this ministry, inquire about the specifics of a Christian small group. There are many good definitions of a Christian small group. For our purposes, it is essential that the definition includes and values a few important descriptors.

1. **Face-to-face** becomes the necessary dynamic for intimate relationships. Each Sunday Christians gather to hear the proclamation of God's Word. There is, however, no opportunity to raise the hand and ask for a further explanation. We all sit in rows and face the back of another person's head. There is a basic understanding that the average person retains only 10 percent, at best, of what they hear. This statistic increases to a possible 90 percent when hearing and interacting happen together. A small group provides that arena for interactive face-to-face dialogue where the tensions of life and faith interact.

2. **Three to twelve people** is an important dynamic to remember. The low number often reflects the purpose of the group as accountability driven. Three is a healthy grouping for this purpose. Surpassing twelve for nurture groups creates difficulty in achieving trusting relationships and opportunities for each person to be heard. Jesus set an excellent example with his group of twelve. Multiplying the group, however, needs to be considered when the magical number of twelve is exceeded.

3. Regular basis is critical for the group in order to form increasing trust levels with one another. Making the small group a priority is essential as is the frequency of the scheduled meetings. When new groups start, once a week is a powerful beginning. Some groups, when established, will switch to twice a month or three weeks on and one week off. Groups, such as fellowship groups meeting once a month, lose the opportunity for developing the trust level that creates intimate relationships for healthy spiritual growth.

4. Particular purpose drives the vision of the small group. There must be a reason for the meetings and goals need to be determined. When a group is begun, the vision for spiritual growth, accountability, mission, or task becomes the anchor for the defining ingredients. It is in the design of the purpose and guidelines of the group that the original Old Testament covenantal model is represented. There are important ingredients of small group life that need to be understood and included in the design of the group. In our chapter on covenants, we will explore the process more thoroughly.

5. Honoring God, growing spiritually, and **connecting with others** is modeled in the early history of the Christian church. In Acts chapter 2 and 4, we see examples of worship, nurture, fellowship, and mission that were basic to their life together. These elements become an integral part of the small group life. The Bible challenges us to strive for holiness, to grow in our faith, to love one another, to connect with His family for meaningful relationships and accountability.

6. Reaching out to those in need is an important function of a healthy small group. The mission of a small group should always include providing for the needs represented within the small group members. Reaching out to those within the larger church family and witnessing for Christ in the community needs to happen for a group to remain vibrant. The popular open chair concept should be included from time to time for those anxious to join groups or for introducing Christ to those who are seeking. All facets of group life are important to keep the group in healthy community. When one aspect is overlooked, the life of the group becomes less effective.

HOW SMALL GROUPS SHOULD FUNCTION

As we think of the varying descriptors in the small group definition, it is important to take a look at the ingredients of small group life. Healthy small groups should have a balance of caring, growing, and doing. We observe in the life of the early church that "believers devoted themselves to the apostles' teaching and to the fellowship, to the breaking of bread and to prayer ... they gave to anyone as he had need ... they broke bread in their homes and ate together with glad and sincere hearts, praising God and enjoying the favor of all the people." And ... "the Lord added to their number daily those who were being saved" (Acts 2:42-47). If you include caring, growing, and doing in your group as you begin your life together, you will be blessed as well.

1. Caring for one another by coming together intentionally as a small group allows the experience of common unity in Christ. It is here that relationships develop to become significantly more than superficial conversations and friendly "hellos" of a larger gathering. The small group provides the environment for not only learning more of God's plan for our lives, but creates the venue for knowing each other through shared lives and story telling. The fellowship involved in this interaction deepens the care and connection; love is expressed and lives celebrated. Through prayer and worship members are supported, lives are transformed, and God is honored. Pastoral staff cannot care for every member of the congregation, but being part of a healthy small group can provide most of the care that is needed.

2. Growing spiritually should be a goal of every small group member. As we observe in Acts chapter 2, the early church devoted themselves to the apostles' teaching. How much time do we devote in our busy days to Bible study, silence and reflection? The small group is a place where this can happen on a regular basis. We should have a hunger for God's Word, a willingness to submit to its authority and a desire to glorify God. Coming together to study God's Word nurtures our lives, helps us to grow in authentic Christian community and allows the Holy Spirit to make those necessary defining life changes. Growing develops opportunities not only for loving, knowing, serving, and celebrating one another, but admonishing when necessary.

3. Doing becomes the application of our learning experience within the small group. It is often stated that any small group existing for a period of time without becoming involved in occasional mission, will eventually become ingrown and ineffective. I have certainly found that to be true. An outward expression of the Christian faith through caring and loving acts for those in need (materially or spiritually) is essential. Becoming an isolated clique is not the goal of small groups, but extending beyond the confines of the group and

into a needy world becomes a biblical response to the many one another mandates. The options are numerous and diverse. Be open for opportunities to help
not only one another in the small group, but also to reach out to neighbors in
need, meet a particular request of the church family, or issue an invitation to
those who do not know Christ to be introduced to Christianity.

Looking back at the Acts chapter 2 passage again, why did the early church
grow at such a rapid rate? Apparently the disciples obeyed Jesus' command, "A
new command I give you: Love one another. As I have loved you, so you must
love one another. By this all men will know that you are my disciples, if you love
one another" (John 13:34-35).

In his book, The Rise of Christianity, professor Rodney Stark presents many
variables that contributed to the development of the Christian faith.[24] There
are several noteworthy points from his work that are instructive as we reflect
on the beginning of the Christian faith and church. As we are told in Scripture,
the starting number mentioned in Acts 1:14-15 was 120; in Acts 2:41, 3,000 were
added; in Acts 4:4 the number grew to 5,000; and in Acts 21:20, by the sixth
decade of the first century, there were "many thousands of Jews" in Jerusalem
who believed. Stark writes that these later figures possibly were figures of
speech and "only meant to render impressive the marvel that here the Lord
himself is at work."[25]

From his significant research, Stark estimates that a 40 percent increase
per decade (or 3.2 percent per year) seems the most plausible estimate of the
growth rate of Christianity during the first several centuries.[26] During this span
of time the church met in homes yet remained an open network, able to keep
building bonds with outsiders, rather than becoming a closed community of
believers. And from the start, Christian doctrine absolutely prohibited abortion
and infanticide (which were prevalent practices and significant methods used
in controlling gender and population in the culture), classifying both as murder. These moral issues were instrumental in the increasing numbers of new

---

24 Rodney Stark, The Rise of Christianity (Harper: San Francisco, 1997). This is an excellent source for important cultural issues leading to the impressive initial growth of the
Christian faith. Using many resources of original form and current research, Stark inte-
grates his own research to complement the larger picture. The book is most helpful in
understanding the life and culture through primary sources. Stark is professor of sociolo-
gy and comparative religion at Baylor University.

25 Ibid., 3.

26 Ibid., 6.

believers. Note Stark's comments concerning the belief and behavior of the Christians at that time:

"Christianity revitalized life in Greco-Roman cities by providing new norms and new kinds of social relationships able to cope with many urgent urban problems. To cities filled with the homeless and impoverished, Christianity offered charity as well as hope. To cities filled with newcomers and strangers, Christianity offered an immediate basis for attachments. To cities filled with orphans and widows, Christianity provided a new and expanded sense of family. To cities torn by violent ethnic strife, Christianity offered a new basis for social solidarity (cf. Pelikan 1987:21). And to cities faced with epidemics, fires, and earthquakes, Christianity offered effective nursing services."[27] "For a group to grow as rapidly as Christians did, it must maintain close ties to nonmembers - it must remain an open network. A truly underground Christianity would have remained insignificant."[28]

Understanding the Greco-Roman culture at that time helps to understand how strategic and powerful the Christian witness and life became. The behavior of Christians that Stark recounts was radical behavior and not the norm. We learn today from these ageless examples the value of loving one another, building relationships with God and others, and to reaching out to those in need.

Through this revealing historical recount, here in the twenty-first century, we continue to observe how they loved one another, how empowered they were by being identified with Jesus Christ and how their lives were radically transformed by the Holy Spirit. They saw hope, joy, peace, and shared love as those with needs were served. They certainly had their problems, but the model that Jesus gives to us through them has passed the test of time and God is using it powerfully today. When small groups are healthy small groups, others want to join, groups multiply, disciples are made, and churches are renewed.

One more defining element needs to be emphasized about community. We need to differentiate between Christian community and community in general. The word common is the basis for community that means something is shared. For instance, the historic Boston Common in Boston, Massachusetts, now a

---

27 Ibid., 161.
28 Ibid., 193.

beautiful park, was once the first common ground for anyone to graze their animals or plant their gardens. It was a gathering place for neighbors to connect and build relationships. We all have community gatherings of some sort in our neighborhoods, towns, and cities. Small groups gather for all sorts of purposes that might not have a spiritual focus at all. One purpose of this manual is to challenge you to pray for an authentic spiritual community where individual Christian lives are inspected through God's lens, where we stand in awe of God, where God's Word is acted upon, where a safe place is formed, where each one is honored, where trust develops, love is expressed, joys are shared, grieving is allowed, and lives are open for change. That's a tall order. But with God's grace and through authentic community, our hearts and souls will yearn for God's renewal.

Larry Crabb challenges us to think about our spiritual life as two rooms. One room we become very comfortable in because we choose how to organize and furnish it. The second room, the upper room, he explains, is God's room, a place where God furnishes and organizes and where, unfortunately we are less comfortable.[29] The challenge for us is to strive to live in the upper room that can only be achieved by being in a supportive spiritual community. It is often easy to be part of a small group that never travels around the bases of small group life, where masks are worn and fears and insecurities are concealed. This is not authentic spiritual community! Our goal is to be powerfully enabled by the Holy Spirit to create a safe place for accountability, for spiritual formation, and for modeling Christ throughout life experiences. Small groups are also powerful venues for leadership development, so be on the watch for those who might step up to the plate with an opportunity to expand the ministry.

And, keep in mind, if new people coming into your church are not connected fairly quickly, they will go where they can be connected or not go at all. Unfortunately many churches do not have a ministry of connection in place for new people looking for community and relationships.

Overlooking these various strategic formats for caring, connecting, and building relationships through authentic Christian community weakens the church. Church pastors cannot care and relate to everyone in the church family. The small group becomes the framework for meaningful relationships, where everybody knows your name and cares to grow spiritually with you. So, whatever style group you wish to create, whatever you decide to call it, there is huge

---

29 Crabb, 59-71.

potential to influence the life of the church through this nucleus of a few gathered people Caring, Growing and Doing together.

Leadership is critical to the life of the group. As we travel through this training material, many concepts and skills will be addressed. Our next chapter is designed to help you understand the criterion for being a leader who models Christ, motivates the members, and utilizes skills for creating healthy small groups.

Please prepare the following Bible study. Experiencing group interaction and sharing the leadership role will reinforce the concepts presented. As a response to this chapter, be thinking about the steps you will take for building authentic Christian community in your new or existing group.

CREATING HEALTHY COMMUNITY

I. TELL

- » Briefly describe a small group experience that made you feel like you really belonged. What would you define as the important ingredient for making you feel comfortable and welcomed?
- » Briefly describe a time when you saw someone in need and gave, perhaps sacrificially, a possession of yours to help out. What were some of your reservations? Emotions? Responses?

2. DISCUSS

The contents of this chapter should provide opportunities for significant discussion and personal story telling concerning the power of achieving authentic Christian community, the getting to know you process. In what ways has this chapter influenced you for creating caring and trusting relationship?

THE BELIEVERS SHARE THEIR POSSESSIONS

Read Acts 4:32-37

3. SCRIPTURE

The early church had recently experienced the coming of the Holy Spirit. We see the Holy Spirit's powerful transformation of the twelve disciples from their prior walking wounded condition to confident, bold believers. They continued meeting together, praying, reflecting on the Apostles' teaching, enabling them to blend their belief and behavior. They seem to be depicting the priestly prayer in John 17 when Jesus asked the Father for love and unity of all believers. In the Acts chapter 4 passage, the doing part of spiritual community is apparent. We can learn from these first Christians as we observe how they demonstrated their love and care for one another.

Look (observation)

- » Describe the new believer's attitude and its effect on one another. What qualities were reflected in this emerging community of believers?
- » Several of the new believers were financially sound. What was the

motivation for them to give so generously? In what way did this action build up their body of believers?

» In response to their compassion and unity, what was the result in their ministry?

Think (interpretation)

» Describe the clear principle Scripture is stating in this passage.
» Luke singled out Barnabas as an example. Think about the implications of this at that time and what you know about Barnabas' future. What comes to mind?
» What does this early church mission imply for our church/small groups today?

Act (application)

» If your group were to copy Barnabas' example, what would it look like?
» If you are interested in leading a small group, how do you see healthy small groups making a change in your church through meaningful community? Give an example of a possibility or something that you have already experienced.
» Recalling various Scripture examples for helping those in need, in what way can you show Christian generosity to someone this week? If nothing comes to mind, keep your eyes and hearts open for an opportunity!

4. PRAYER

Before you leave the group, pray for one another. Pray for your future group. Ask God to help you create a caring, loving, relational spiritual community where, through God's grace, life-transformation will happen.

5. PREPARATION

Identify the discussion leader for your next meeting. During the week, read the chapter on Leadership and prepare the small group Bible study. Doing the study each week will help you model and observe the learning curve of leading well.

"They devoted themselves to the apostles' teaching and to the fellowship, to the breaking of read and to prayer. Everyone was filled with awe, and many wonders and miraculous signs were done by the apostles. All the believers were together and had everything in common. Selling their possessions and goods, they gave to anyone as he had need. Every day they continued to meet together in the temple courts. They broke bread in their homes and ate together with glad and sincere hearts, praising God and enjoying the favor of all the people. And the Lord added to their number daily those who were being saved."

Acts 2:42-47

3

LEADERSHIP: MAKING AN IMPACT

"Spiritual leadership is moving people on to God's agenda."

Henry Blackaby, *Spiritual Leadership*

Think about leadership, the lessons you've learned and the impact those experiences made on you. Perhaps one incident stands out among many. For me that experience happened when I was fourteen years old and at a summer camp I had attended for three years in a row. I was the camp bugler which meant I was up earlier than others, warmed my face up to blow warnings, revelry, meals, to the colors, rest hour, and taps. It was a large camp and I had three stations from which to toot my horn! Throughout the summer I had anticipated being asked back the following year as a counselor in training. That's the prize. That's what every camper hopes to achieve. Life at camp was diverse and one of the activities I came to love was sailing. Suddenly I found myself doing well, racing often, and missing more than a few of my bugle calls.

As the last day of camp arrived, my friends were approached by the camp director and offered a position in the counselor program the following summer.

The director did not seek me out. Certainly, I thought, it would happen before I left camp. As I packed up to return home I thought, certainly I will receive a letter. I did not! With careful strokes, I constructed a letter to the director describing my love for the camp and my desire for the counselor-in-training program. I was stunned with her reply. I was not being asked back. Her words ripped through me as she stated I could not be trusted. To her I had failed in my commitment with my bugling responsibilities and therefore could not be considered for potential leadership. I would not become a counselor-in-training. Sting. Disappointment. Agony. I still think of the humility, embarrassment, the loss and grieving. The experience has stayed with me all these many years and I know without a doubt that my focus and total commitment to that which I agree to do throughout these years, was a direct result of this camp disappointment. It made a huge impact.

DEFINING LEADERSHIP

There are many excellent definitions of leadership. One night while driving, I heard an interview with a woman who held the position of principal viola with the Boston Symphony Orchestra. The principal player is responsible for leading his or her section. When asked what her most difficult part of the responsibility was, she stated it was leading her group and being led by the conductor at the same time. It paints a picture of the necessity for each of us, as we lead others, to keep our eyes on the One who is worthy of following: God! For our purposes, I like the definition of leadership offered by Henry Blackaby: "spiritual leadership is moving people on to God's agenda."[30]

As leaders we will leave a legacy one way or another. Therefore, leading others, yet being led while keeping our eyes on our heavenly Father, becomes essential for moving people into God's agenda: to be imitators of him (Ephesians 5:1). Certainly this kind of leadership makes an impact on others spiritually and beckons each of us toward God and His desire for our lives.

LEARNING FROM JESUS

One of the early lessons we learn from Jesus is that he did only what his Father told him to do. Constantly Jesus responded to the desires of God through his intimate relationship in prayer and daily communion with his Father. We can

---

30 Henry Blackaby and Richard Blackaby, Spiritual Leadership (Nashville, Tennessee: Broadman and Holman Publishers, 2001), 20.

benefit from Jesus' example, as we too need to keep our eyes on our heavenly Father, striving to be in His will and doing His purpose. Paul writes "Be imitators of God, therefore, as dearly loved children and live a life of love, just as Christ loved us and gave himself up for us as a fragrant offering and sacrifice to God" (Ephesians 5:1-2).

Jesus was a leader who prepared his small discipleship group to be disciplined, strategic, committed leaders. Jesus took the initiative and time to speak, model, share, equip, and encourage his diverse friends. Jesus was a servant by nature. In his humility, Jesus demonstrated what servanthood looked like and challenged his followers to be and do the same. This form of servant leadership is our challenge today.

The training of the twelve was a slow process. It seemed as if they would never learn, but it all came together for them as teaching and experience, wrapped together with the power of the Holy Spirit, enabled Jesus' disciples to birth the Christian church. Observing the life of Jesus helps to challenge and inform us as we prepare to lead with excellence. Just what did he do and how did he do it?

THE PATTERN JESUS CREATED

First and foremost, Jesus was in constant communion with the Father. Stating that he could do nothing outside the Father's plan (John 5:19), Jesus acknowledged the source of his wisdom and strength. Being empowered, he led his group where he wanted them to go by words and action. Sharing himself, Jesus modeled humility, love, trust, and companionship as he created his spiritual community of twelve. When Jesus wanted to teach a lesson, he told a story, modeled the action, encouraged, and corrected when necessary. Throughout the demanding schedule and busyness of life, Jesus always took time to go to a quiet place and pray to his Father (Mark 1:35). Communion with God the Father through prayer and solitude was the source of Jesus' strength, wisdom, and power for leading his group and doing God's will.

When Jesus said "follow me," he called his group into servant action. In spite of their weaknesses and failures, the Holy Spirit brought them into new power and confidence on the day of Pentecost. As Jesus calls us to follow, we too can experience this same power as we live our lives and lead others. However, stepping up to the plate of small group leadership is more than deciding it might be a fun thing to do. We influence people one way or another and it is our Christian responsibility to be well-prepared vessels whom God is pleased to use. God has given us a powerful privilege in allowing us to be involved with the process of life-transformation.

MAKING AN IMPACT

At one of our church leadership celebration events, the speaker, Dr. Gary Parrett, a professor at Gordon-Conwell Theological Seminary, used an acrostic that was very helpful for the challenge of leadership and I have continue to use his idea in varying formats. It is a challenge to leaders and ambassadors of Christ to lead with excellence and authenticity. As we examine the essence of spiritual leadership, take inventory of how the following suggestions might affect your life. (The original acrostic has been modified.) As leaders, we need to stay on the growing edge of maturing in our biblical knowledge and act on that knowledge as we put our faith into practice. Leading with spiritual excellence will **IMPACT** those who attend our small groups.

I. INTEGRITY

"In everything, set them an example
by doing what is good.
In your teaching, show integrity."

Titus 2:7

To use the common expression, we need to "walk our talk." A lack of integrity has no place as we follow Christ in leadership. Integrity means to be integrated, to form or to blend. We are called to blend our belief and our behavior in modeling Christ. There can be no gap between how we challenge our group and the way we respond personally to that challenge. The person of integrity is one in whom the Spirit has blended belief and behavior in order to produce consistency. As leaders, called by God for His purpose, morality must be found in our behavior. Integrity demands integrating scriptural faith and action in the home, in the marketplace, and in the neighborhood. God is the author of truth, and there is no place for us in His work if integrity is not exemplified as we strive to lead others. We might think of integrity as "holiness, set apart for God's use."

Integrity is one of the most complimentary attributes one can acquire. Integrity comes with humility before God with open hearts and minds earnestly desiring His power of renewal.

2. MODEL CHRIST

> "Be imitators of God ... live a life of love."
>
> *Ephesians 5:1*

The tense of this verb "be" is imperative making this verse not a suggestion, but a command. We are to act just as Christ acted. Therefore, it becomes necessary to know the heart beat of Jesus in order to imitate God. It means concerted effort to read, study, know, reflect, and act upon the truth of Scripture. It means to respond to life and chaotic experiences as Jesus did. It means the right use of knowledge.

The once popular movement, "what would Jesus do?" (WWJD), sends a good message, but only has worth if people take the time to actually learn and imitate what Jesus would have done had the situation been similar. We need to be knowledgeable of and sensitized to God's Word, allowing Him to change us to live moment to moment in integrity as imitators of Christ in all our thoughts and actions. If we become imitators of God, we allow God's Word to create in us new hearts that respond with better choices. "The heart, the inner life, shaped primarily by trust, molds our motives. Our motives establish our values. And our values govern our actions. What we believe about ourselves takes root and is nourished in our hearts. And it's from the heart that our destiny, our ultimate influence and value flows."[31]

3. PRAYER

> "Be joyful always, pray continually."
>
> *1 Thessalonians 5:16-17*

---

31 Bill Thrall, Bruce McNicol and Ken McElrath, The Ascent of a Leader (San Francisco, California: Jossey-Bass, 1999), 63.

Prayer happens in various ways for each person. Whatever form or model you prefer, Paul challenged the Thessalonians and challenges us today to have prayer as the foundation for all we become and attempt to do for Christ. We are to pray continually. Concerning our leadership with small groups, we pray for wisdom, for God's presence and power as we prepare our meetings, and for each person in our group for whom we care. Prayer is where we start, not as an after thought or an SOS as we head into our small group time.

As believers, we know that we can do nothing for God without the Holy Spirit. Therefore it is essential to first seek Him in prayer before we start any process of planning. We model Christ and seek those quiet places, those times of withdrawal, in order to become more intimate with Him. Prayer develops this personal relationship with Christ. The root of intimacy is to be tight, formed, pressed together. How can we do this with a frantic life that is too busy for daily prayer and reflection? Eagerly seek Him in prayer before you attempt to lead your group.

4. ACCOUNTABILITY

"Speaking the truth in love,
we will in all things grow up into him
who is the head, that is, Christ."

Ephesians 4:15

Without a doubt, we will be accountable to God for what we have done and what we have neglected to do. We are commanded to be worthy of our calling, which is in Christ Jesus. In addition, every leader ought to have established a relationship of accountability with another person and definitely with the small group ministry team. We do not lead or learn in isolation. We function as the body of Christ by speaking the truth in love and building each other up to edify the church. Accountability happens before God, within your church ministry, and should be a goal of your small group.

Making sure you include accountability in response to your study is critical, for if we keep an accumulation of fascinating, detailed information in our head and do not move it down twelve inches to our heart, we have lost the value of the study. Implementing accountability to the Scripture you have studied in a sense of "what will we do differently because we have studied this scripture" becomes a defining moment of group time. Effective leaders set the example by allowing themselves to be vulnerable through accountability.

5. CULTIVATE YOUR SOUL

"Train yourself to be godly."

1 Timothy 4:7

To cultivate our soul requires a choice to be made. It takes action and time on our part. It translates to having the same intentions as the mind of Christ. Wouldn't it be wonderful if we could acquire this intimacy with Christ by osmosis? However, it takes intentional actions on our part. I struggle with being a task-driven, type-A, often driven person. Sitting quietly before God, or anywhere in fact, is difficult for me. I was powerfully challenged in this area while attending seminary. I always knew about the spiritual disciplines, but avoided getting too close. Prayer was hard for me, let alone all the other time-consuming disciplines that were suggested. Yet, through one of my courses, "Pursuit of Wholeness."[32] God placed before me a new way of life; one that was more endearing to Him and formative in His plan for me. The disciplines I experienced in this course have been made a priority in my life, and God has blessed me greatly through the effort and time. It still does not come easily, yet my intimacy with Christ deepens continually.

Have you taken the time to cultivate your soul through spiritual disciplines? What disciplines do you practice? Leadership requires a consistent prayer life, but what about silence and solitude? These practices allow us the time for quietness before God, a time to listen to Him without interjecting our agenda and a time to reflect on His Word and its implication for our lives. Reflection means to bend back something in order to take a closer look. Sitting quietly before God with a reflective mind and heart cultivates our soul. It digs deeply into our life and prepares our hearts to see and act differently. Slow down and see the moments God has given you. Respond. Let God bless you through them. Take time to listen and reflect.

---

32 Richard Peace, "Pursuit of Wholeness" Gordon-Conwell Theological Seminary course, August 1995.

"Being reflective is a way of life that prepares the heart so something of eternal significance can be planted there."[33]

6. TRUST THE HOLY SPIRIT

"Now to him who is able to do immeasurably more than all we ask or imagine according to his power that is at work within us, to him be glory in the church and in Christ Jesus throughout all generations, forever and ever. Amen."

Ephesians 3:20-21

Trust the Holy Spirit to lead you in your vision and preparation. Trust the Holy Spirit to bear fruit in yourself and in your group. Complete dependence on the Holy Spirit as you prepare for your meeting, for the building of relationships and the group life in general, provides opportunities for life transformation. Remember, we are not the change agents, the Holy Spirit is. Spiritual renewal and life-change happens in Spirit-filled, healthy small groups.

Significant seeds planted in your life have brought you into leadership and now you are planting seeds and leaving a legacy in the lives of others. Leadership is not only a significant responsibility from God, it has the potential of making a huge impact on the life of another person and the church community. Small group leaders can easily learn various skills necessary for leading a small group. However, without building personal Christian character that God expects, our impact will be far less effective. Integrity, modeling Christ, prayer, accountability, cultivating our souls, and trusting the Holy Spirit builds Christian character necessary for influencing others towards God's agenda.

AVOIDING THE PITFALLS

Even with the commitment to develop and lead with Christ-like character, the old human nature rears its ugly head from time to time. Impediments

---

33 Ken Gire, The Reflective Life (Colorado Springs, Colorado: Chariot Victor, 1998), 41.

surface, barriers are created and our default system sides more with the flesh than with the Character of God. Henri Nouwen wrote an entire book concerning the temptations that plagued him as an influential man of God, popular speaker, and professor. This wise and concise book, In The Name of Jesus, challenges the reader with temptations of leadership that create a desire to be relevant, and at the same time, to be spectacular and powerful. Gareth Icenogle, Pastor of the National Presbyterian Church in Washington, D.C., has noted other temptations as well. Be aware of these pitfalls and deal with them wisely before they take hold:

1. SAVIOR OF THE GROUP

The temptation to meet all the needs of the group is an unhealthy and unreachable goal for a leader. We cannot meet all the needs of the group nor should we attempt to try. As leaders we are caring shepherds calling upon other group members to join us in prayer and support for each member. Knowing our strengths and weaknesses empowers us to acknowledge our limitations. Having a prepared list of resources and aids is an important asset for the leader, as often we are unskilled or incapable of helping in specific critical areas. Leaders who feel they need to meet every need most often become over-burdened and a detriment to the group.

2. CONTROL

The temptation to be the group's controlling manager issues surface from time to time. Often this stems from insecurity or pride. Perhaps the pursuit of control gives us a bit more confidence, albeit false confidence, as we lead. It becomes, however, an attitude of power over and suppression of the group. It is a tendency to lead and not be led, or teach and not be open to being taught. It is a desire to call all the shots, meet all the needs of the group and think more highly of ourselves than we ought.

3. THEOLOGICAL EXPERT ROLE

The temptation to serve as the group's sole theological authority[34] is not part of the job description. As small group leaders, we should be growing spiritually alongside our fellow travelers. While we may have had more theological

---

34 Gareth Icenogle, Biblical Foundations for Small Group Ministry (Downers Grove, Illinois: InterVarsity Press, 1994), 173, lists these three temptations.

training or spent more years in biblical study, we do not want to present ourselves as knowing all the answers. In playing the role of theological expert, we
create an environment where group members tend to look to us more than
keeping their eyes on Jesus and God's Word. Being afraid to say "I don't know"
creates an unhealthy small group and sometimes results in the dreaded shared
ignorance. Remember to be honest and promise to find out the answer to
perplexing questions that are not immediately answerable. Or even better, delegate the responsibility to someone in the group.

DEVELOPING SPIRITUAL GIFTS

Small groups can become excellent opportunities for leadership development. Constantly watching for potential leaders is crucial for building a small
group ministry. If leaders continually plan and implement all aspects of group
life, new leaders will not be developed. Jesus' model of leadership development was evident and powerful as he enabled and empowered his disciples
with their leadership experiences. Spiritual gifts will surface when opportunities
to exercise them are available. Some group members are excited to participate
in some sort of leadership, while others are happy to be passive and watch it all
happen. We actually do a disservice to those in our care by not allowing them
to participate in the group leadership process or when we fail to stretch and
push one another in our varied spiritual journeys.

Always be looking for the gifts God has given to your group members.
Consider how you might utilize that person to build up the group. It might
be prayer, worship, facilitating the bible study, hospitality, or some other gift
manifestation. Delegating is critical in healthy group process and you must be
willing to exercise it at the right moment. Don't be threatened by gifted group
members. Stop worrying if the job will be done exactly like what you would
have done and allow others to be part of the process.

KNOWING YOUR STYLE

The type of leadership you exhibit is also an important aspect of leading
with excellence. Leadership styles are commonly grouped into four types: (1)
autocratic, (2) authoritative, (3) democratic, and (4) laissez-faire. Autocratic and
laissez-faire are not effective styles of leadership in developing healthy small
group ownership and team interaction. Using the authoritative style in the early
life-stage of the group and moving into a more democratic style is best.

1. **Autocratic** leadership allows the designated leader to make all the decisions. He or she not only makes all the decisions for the group at the beginning stages, but throughout the life of the small group. Often for the new believer or the passive mature believer, this is an advantage as it results in little to no effort on the part of the group member. However, it hampers the spiritual journeys of most participants, leaving their gifts undetermined and unused. In time, this may result in members dropping out of group life. When this leadership style is in place, control of what happens in group life rests with one person.

Some group members begin to rely too heavily on the leader, allowing the conversation to become dominated by him or her. This results in an unhealthy dynamic. In some cases, this environment could create opportunities for shared ignorance in that the leader feels the need to answer or add to every question whether he or she is prepared properly or not. When the leader does not know the answer, the tendency is to guess. I've seen it happen. I've done it myself and am not proud of how I handled my feelings of inadequacy.

Icenogle states: "a small group cannot be sustained and nurtured to maturity solely through the knowledge and expertise of the leader, but through the leader's willingness to listen to the voice of God and help the group learn to listen and respond to the voice of God... the group leader who listens to the voice of God is the leader who does not lead out of demand but out of loving relationship. The good group leader will not permit the expectations of the group to block out the quiet voice of the Spirit of God."[35]

The temptation is to be a leader who has independent vision and makes independent decision rather than the spiritually growing leader with a servant attitude. When mutuality and interdependence are honored, small group relationships are nurtured and new leadership is developed. The second style of leadership fosters this process.

2. **Authoritative** leadership is an excellent beginning style in healthy small groups. Limited yet flexible structure implies being well prepared. When using this style in the very early stages of group life, the leader is able to keep the group focused on a common vision. Healthy small group process requires good leadership, an ability to move people on to God's agenda. A well-prepared leader sets a few boundaries or expectations and gently persuades those in the

---

35 Ibid,, 173.

group to participate in the process. Once a leader has made enough decisions to give the initial structure, the leader should change their style of leadership and invite more discussion and decision making by the group.

3. **Democratic** leadership considers every member's interests and concerns as decision-making is exercised. The democratic leadership style and attitude that follows the initial authoritative stage encourages others to be participants in the purpose of the group time together. Gradually adjusting to this more democratic style will empower group members to a greater degree and it is here where we start seeing various spiritual gifts surface and new leadership develop.

Leaders should look to the group members for ideas and implementation. It does not mean that the leader does not have input. Remember, leaders are in the process of influencing others, but do so with sensitivity and attempt to involve everyone in the process. That is how ownership of a group is established.

When group members are part of the process, the group identity changes from Peter's group to my group. It is an important step to accomplish. A group can continue in this style of leadership, which is minimal, until the group reaches the end of their time together. In the winding down stage, a leader would be wise in reverting back to more authoritative leadership in order to keep on course and follow through with the vision of the covenant.

The last style of leadership we will explore is most often ineffective and not fair to those who expect and set aside time for meaningful spiritual community.

4. **Laissez-faire** leadership is the least effective style of leadership for small group process. This type of leader basically does not prepare and lets whatever happens happen. How often I have heard, I just let the Holy Spirit lead. We all want the Holy Spirit to lead, but there are leadership expectations for leading well and with excellence if we want to move people on to God's agenda and part of that process is to be grounded in prayer and to have a plan. However, there are times when your well-prepared study may need to be set aside when a member is suffering and needs special attention. That's to be expected from time to time, but not as a weekly routine.

A well prepared leader pours his or her heart into the time together, praying that God would not only bless the meeting and relationships, but also that the Holy Spirit would be at work transforming each and every life. Caring and growing spiritually together is powerful and no small group participant would want the following scenario experience by Mike Shepherd, small group consultant and trainer for many years.

> Have you ever participated in a group meeting that was poorly run? It can drive you nuts! I got stuck in one of those meetings recently when I was asked to evaluate a particular church's group ministry. I went incognito. They had no ideas who I was. It was fun but chaotic to say the least. When I arrived no one greeted me or extended any kind of welcome. I sat down. No one interacted with me. I waited for the meeting to start. It did, about 20 minutes later than it was supposed to. There were no refreshments. The leaders stood up and said, 'Well, what do you guys want to do tonight, anybody have any ideas?' I kid you not. I thought I was in small group hell. It was awful.[36]

Have you experienced a small group with this type of leadership? How compelling was it for you to return? There is no structure, no agenda, nothing in place that attracts or simulates commitment and spiritual growth. This leadership style defies the description of a Christian small group that was discussed in Chapter Two, Community. Yes, all leaders should be sensitive to the leading of the Holy Spirit. Habitually utilizing a style reflecting "let's see what happens tonight" neglects the healthy and proper preparation for your time together.

BUILDING A TEAM

If one of the goals of small group process is practicing mutual and interdependent behavior, each group needs a designated leader willing to do the initial preparation and provide proper leadership. Being aware of his or her leadership abilities, the leader needs to be willing to give ownership of group life to members along the way. As we build up one another in Christ, we build each other into a team. The leader must model dependency on the Holy Spirit, recognizing his or her strengths and weaknesses, seeking the life-change goal, and striving to implement the leadership development potential within a given group. In other words, the leader needs not only to lead, but to be willing to learn along with the group.

---

36 Mike Shepherd, "Strategic Group Meetings," [small group article on-line], April 2001, http://www.smallgroups.com,. Smallgroups.com is a most informative website for small group process. With minimum membership fee, one is able to read relevant, instructive, fun and encouraging articles. Each month various topics of small group life are explored.

Remember the comment from the principal viola player of the Boston Symphony: the challenge is to lead while being led. The leader needs to let go and give responsibilities to others if new leaders are to be developed. This, by the way, becomes a powerful influence in preparing for future ministry by multiplying small groups. And remember, the best design for small group leadership is to have a co-leader or an apprentice. The difference being that a co-leader is usually experienced and an apprentice is learning to lead by observing the leader. If you happen to be leading alone, keep an eye out for someone to fill the co-leader or apprentice spot.

Concerning leadership, a lesson I learned quite impressively while in seminary happened in a leadership seminar. I had been involved in various leadership roles from a very early age. Now as a driven ministry leader, I was nearly over-committed with church responsibilities, including a young Pioneer Girls group consisting of forty church and school friends of my daughters. I spent the summer planning the year. I had each week outlined as to worship, lesson, projects, crafts, and field trips. As I met with my team, I presented the year's schedule and felt as if I had given them a tremendous gift of leadership. I did most of the preparation and implementation. Suddenly, through this leadership seminar, a light dawned! I had been doing such a disservice to my team. I had made it easy for them, but I failed to develop leaders. I wasn't working myself out of a job. I knew what I wanted to see happen and how it would happen.

Delegating leadership can be difficult in that people don't always do assignments the way you might have done them. As I committed to sharing the planning and implementation, I began to see their confidence surface. We brainstormed, I let them make more decisions (which, by the way, were often better than those I would have made) and we became a team. Utilizing the concepts and skills I was acquiring in my class, I also asked for honest evaluation and suggestions to improve my leadership style in hopes of stretching not only me, but also my friends around the table.

INCLUDING EVALUATION

If we are committed to learning as we lead, evaluation is important in the process. Assessment is a necessary on-going aspect of small group leadership. As you continue to experience small group leadership, take inventory of your abilities. Identify your strengths and weaknesses. If you are unsure, your group can help you out! It's a worthwhile practice. The evaluation process is all part of the accountability of leadership. Having others reflect on your gifts and style allows for honest reflection and helps to create a mindset of leading with excellence. Negative feedback is difficult to receive without trying to justify your actions, but becomes the growing edge of improvement. As you begin to share the leadership responsibilities, evaluation becomes an important part of encouraging and stretching those who agree to the responsibility of leading.

According to the evaluation, what changes can be made in the style of leadership that would be beneficial to the group process? Understanding autocratic, authoritative, democratic, and laissez-faire styles provides a grid for our personal evaluation and how we as leaders are moving our members on to God's agenda. As leaders, we are wise to consider and understand each style and its implications before we begin leading for the first time. In time, look for areas of small group life that you can delegate to capable people in your group.

Remember the example of Moses in Chapter Two on Community? The Jethro principle of delegation is worth remembering. If you are already leading a group, construct a similar chart with small group process responsibilities appropriate for our time and culture. In how many boxes do you find your name?[37]

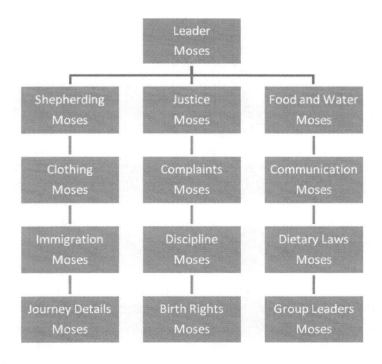

---

37 Thom Corrigan, Pilgrimage Training Group (Littleton, Colorado). Chart is modified from the resource used for small group training seminars, 1995.

SEEING YOURSELF AS A LEADER

Since healthy small group leadership is so strategic in the life of a church, no one wants to end up in a group led in a laissez-faire style by an unprepared leader. It's such a wasted opportunity. If you are directing a small group ministry, you want to create an atmosphere where people recognize that it is a privilege to be asked to lead. If you are a small group leader, I can only guess that your response was: I'm not qualified. In anticipation of this response, it is helpful to look at basic requirements when one considers being a small group leader. No seminary degrees necessary here!

1. CHURCH MEMBERSHIP

First, most often church membership is the first requirement. In some cases, being in agreement with the statement of faith is sufficient. In my experience at our city church where fifty percent of the congregation transitions every two years or less, many experienced and gifted small group leaders did not become members for their short period of time in the area. Through interviews, testimonies, and getting to know each individual, we felt confident in making a decision to invite them into leadership.

Secondly, any potential small group leader should have had experience within the small group context as a participant. If a person expressed an interest in leadership very early in the process of interviewing, I wanted to hear about their small group experiences in the past. If a potential leader has not experienced a small group, it is always wise to suggest joining a group as a participant before pursuing the leadership role. It is here, once again, that initial leadership development occurs as group members have opportunities to lead in various and diverse ways.

2. UNDERSTANDING BIBLICAL PRINCIPLES AND A DESIRE TO GROW AND LEARN

Each leader needs to have a good grasp of the Gospel message. Finding time on a daily basis to read and reflect on God's Word is essential. As leaders, we look to grow spiritually along with our group. Seeking God's will through personal prayer and study is critical for the journey to spiritual maturity. Being a humble, caring, relational person, with the desire to grow spiritually and in service to others is a mark of biblical leadership.

Part of the growing and learning process is recognizing and accepting our strengths and weaknesses. Remember Moses' situation as he tried to hear and solve everyone's problems. God uses each of us in our diversity and through various God-given gifts or acquired skills, we can minister in different ways to our diverse group. Knowing where we are strong allows us to excel in particular areas. It doesn't mean we do everything ourselves, however, as delegation, modeling, and encouragement are essential for leader development among the entire group.

Knowing our weaknesses prevents us from trying to do everything ourselves. In our honesty, it is far wiser to delegate responsibilities to others who seem to be more efficient in particular areas. We cannot do all and be all as leaders of a small group, nor is it healthy. The excitement of diversity reinforces the fact that we are part of the body of Christ, each and every one contributing to the small group experience. Strive to be a servant leader and to know your strengths and weakness. Macchia states: "When we can identify the obstacles that keep us from living out true service, we are cleaner, clearer vessels for the outflow of the love of Christ. When that occurs, we know with certainty that we are thriving in our service."[38]

3. UNDERSTANDING THE COMMITMENT

If you are participating in several ministries and leading a small group is "just one more thing to do," please stop and carefully evaluate whether the time is right for you. Seek spiritual discernment by praying through your schedule to see where the time you have and the gifts you offer seem to fit best. If the call is right for you, clear space in your schedule to be a caring shepherd through the choice of small group leadership. And remember, small group leaders become strategic in the community life and therefore the spiritual growth of the church. It's a huge privilege and responsibility that results in mixed emotions including great excitement, joy, frustration, feeling of defeat, anxious moments, thrills beyond expectations, and empowerment you never thought possible! It is important that you understand the commitment you are making. You will have the responsibility for planning the meeting, preparing the lesson, and (very critical to the health and purpose of your group) caring for those who attend.

---

38 Stephen A Macchia, Becoming a Healthy Disciple: Ten Traits of a Vital Christian (Grand Rapids: Baker Books, 2004), 133-134. This is an important resource developed from Becoming a Healthy Church. An excellent small group Bible study guide is available for discipleship. Macchia presently serves as President, Leadership Transformations, Inc.

You are responsible to God for what He is entrusting to you. We do everything to glorify Him, not ourselves. We do this in His power and for His sake. If you have someone overseeing the small group ministry in your church, you are responsible to that person for following through with the agreed commitment. Learn to be a team player and don't strive to do your own thing with your small group. Remember, too, that your commitment will most likely involve additional meetings for encouragement and for accountability. They are important coaching and learning times and should not be ignored.

Little measures like calling when someone has been absent, sending a card to celebrate a birthday, or meeting for coffee just to hang-out, all become instrumental in creating a strong bond for building relationships and spiritual growth. Commit to personal spiritual growth as you model Christ. Pray, prepare, be excited about God's Word, and be blessed as you serve in this life-transforming ministry.

A FEW REMINDERS

In building a caring spiritual community, the importance of knowing and being known, loving and being loved, serving and being served is essential. As you lead other people into self-disclosure, you need to let your group know the real you. Don't be wearing a mask that says, I have it all together. Identify with them and be one of them as you journey together in spiritual renewal. Encourage them, and love them like Christ loves you; as is. Ask for help when you need it, don't be afraid to say I don't know, be a good listener, be available, and learn the skills for leading and preparing with excellence. Be excited about God's Word and its influence in your life and watch how contagious your love for God becomes! We can learn all the skills necessary for group process, but if we don't lead with authentic Christian character, our influence in leading others on to God's agenda, to be imitators of God, becomes ineffective.

Be prepared, know your skills, let the Holy Spirit do the changing and remember ... as a leader, you will leave a legacy one way or another.

Our next chapter will discuss the importance of intentionally identifying the goals and purposes that drive the life and design of the small group that you will be leading. Please prepare the following small group exercise for your next meeting.

SERVANT LEADERSHIP

1. TELL

» Who has been a significant influence in your life and what was it about that person that recalls powerful memories?

» Sometimes we learn through negative experiences. Have you been involved in ministry where the leader's character, style, or commitment was a barrier to you? If so, in what ways did that experience encourage you to lead differently?

» Think about a serving experience when you thought you performed a humiliating task. What emotions did you experience and what did you learn?

2. DISCUSS

Now that you have explored the characteristics of good leadership and identified some new ideas you might utilize, briefly discuss an area of leadership where you have been challenged and where you feel less comfortable. Comment on ideas in the material that have been new and helpful to you.

JESUS WASHES HIS DISCIPLES' FEET

Read John 13:1-17

3. SCRIPTURE

Jesus' ministry, as the disciples knew it, was coming to an end. They have followed Jesus' requests and have gathered in Jerusalem for the celebration of the Passover Feast. The command to love was not new to them. Jesus, however, turns their concept of love upside down as he gives them an example of God's humble, servant love, showing what is expected of believers who love in Jesus' name and who are called to be his ambassadors of truth.

Look (observation)

» What time of year was it? What do you know about this feast?
» Where does the narration take place? Who is there? What time of day?
» What do you know about foot washing in Jesus' day?

» What did Peter declare he would never do? How did he change his mind?
» What did Jesus ask his disciples to do?

Think (interpretation)

» What does Jesus want his disciples to learn from foot washing?
» Why does Jesus stress the role of the servant in this text?
» What comparison is Jesus making for his disciples about leadership and authority in the kingdom of God and leadership and authority in the world?

Act (application)

» Put yourself in the place of Jesus' disciples. What emotions might have been going through your mind as you realized what Jesus was about to do? Briefly describe how you think you would have responded.
» In what way does this passage challenge you concerning your role as a Christian leader in the home, church, or marketplace?
» Jesus demonstrated unconditional love. We all know people who we think are hard to love. Who comes to mind for you? In what way can you show this person the love of Christ this week?

4. PRAYER

Small group leadership experiences are not all perfect. We often have difficult personalities who seem to sabotage our group purposes. We, in our human nature, do not love everyone as we should. Often, without thinking about it, we place a higher importance on ourselves, or those like us, than those who are hard to love. Pray that the Holy Spirit would fill you with humble love for people who are hard to love naturally. It's amazing what happens. Concerning being servant leaders, Jesus tells his disciples "Now that you know these things, you will be blessed" (John 13:17). You will be blessed as well.

5. PREPARATION

Select the discussion leader for your next meeting. Read the chapter on covenants and complete the Bible study. Pray for one another throughout the week.

"We were not looking for praise from men,
not from you or anyone else. As apostles of Christ
we could have been a burden to you,
but we were gentle among you, like a mother
caring for her little children.
We loved you so much that we were delighted
to share with you not only the gospel of God
but our lives as well, because you had become
so dear to us."

1 Thessalonians 2:6-8

CHAPTER

4

THE COVENANT:
DESIGNING THE GROUP

*"Beginnings are important.
They establish foundations for what is to come."*

Julie Gorman, *Community That Is Christian*

Anyone who has ever been part of a small group most likely has had both positive and negative group experiences. What comes to mind for you? Thinking back to one particular small group my husband and I attended still sends shivers down my spine. It was the first time we had attended this small group. Five minutes into our time together, we knew we had made a horrible mistake. Having agreed to be part of the group for however long, we were reluctant to make a hasty decision to quit before the evening was completed. After sitting on an overstuffed couch between two other people, listening to forty-five minutes of a monotone voice in lecture with no interaction, and realizing our bodies were adversely reacting to the meandering cats, our expectations of small groups became minimal at best. The group meeting ended an hour and a half later than the designated time. We thought that surely this first meeting wouldn't be indicative of the next one. But that was not to be the case, and after a respectable segment of time, our decision not to continue proved to be difficult and awkward for the leader and other members, for we had been friends for several years and anticipated enjoying time together. Not a positive experience.

Sometime later we were asked to form a group with two other couples. One of the members had extensive training in small group process and began discussing the possibilities of our covenant. This sounded much too structured for me, yet it appeared to be the perfect avenue in which we, as individuals, could express the personal goals each of us had for spending time together. With building enthusiasm, we constructed guidelines, purposes, and challenges for our future sessions. We ended our time enjoying the investment and ownership in our new small group. Definitely a positive experience.

It is essential that a small group make decisions together about group life. Goals, format, meeting time, and study need to be agreed upon. Call it a contract or call it a covenant, but understand its implications as a promise and agreement between group members. The word covenant is the word used in the Old and New Testaments when God made a promise or an agreement with His people. The covenant reminds us that God is not only a witness to the agreement, but He is the central person in the agreement and in the group. Understanding the biblical basis for and implementation of a covenant provides the foundation for designing a covenant specific to a particulate group.

Throughout Scripture the development of covenants between God and His people may be seen. Originated by God for man's best interest as he journeyed through life, covenants became agreements between God and man, or more specifically, they were unfailing promises of God to man. One important characteristic of covenants that becomes evident is that God never breaks His covenantal promises, yet man is quite quick to do so. God's Word, promise, or covenant cannot fail. "I will not violate my covenant or alter what my lips have uttered" (Psalm 89:34).

Originally the idea of a covenant was not a religious agreement. It was a concept transferred from ordinary life into the religious sphere. Anything agreed upon by two nations or two persons was a covenant. Often in these covenants or contracts, God came as a third party; the Guardian of the contract.

As we take a closer look at some examples of God's covenants, we observe how God spoke to individuals who would in time represent God's chosen people as a group and gratefully, generations later, we too have become recipients of His glorious and saving promises.

1. ADAM

In the beginning, Adam and his offspring were to be the recipient of God's covenant of ceaseless friendship and intimate relationship; upon Adam's obedience, he would receive the resulting promise of life and blessings (Genesis 1:28-30). That was before the fall. The covenant was altered and new conditions and promises were established (Genesis 3:16-19); yet today we, as recipients, continue to look to the fulfillment when we come face to face with our Lord and Savior.

2. NOAH

With trust and obedience in preparation for survival, Noah entered into a covenant with God following the great flood (Genesis 6:18, 9:8-17). Here God promised that, with the new establishment of His people, there would never be another flood that covered the earth as Noah and his family had experienced. We regularly are reminded of God's faithfulness as we glance at spectacular rainbows from time to time.

3. ABRAHAM

The Lord told Abraham to go to the land that would be shown to him. Leaving extended family, friends, and all with which he was familiar, Abraham began his journey to a new and unknown land. Abraham became the recipient of God's promise that his descendents would be made into a great nation, that Abraham would be blessed, his name made great, and that God would protect him through the process (Genesis 12:1-3). God commanded obedience on the part of Abraham and God's future nation, as they would become God's own people. Lovingly God warned them concerning the dangerous implications of their future disobedience.

4. MOSES

Using every excuse he could verbalize, Moses attempted to suggest that God could find a more gifted person for the task God had set before Moses. Yet God, in his power and faithfulness, chose Moses to lead his people to their new land

and their new status as a nation set apart for God. Moses became the intercessor between God and the people of Israel. His role as a prophet stands out in superlatives to other prophets. Although he did not experience life in the Promised Land, Moses' faithful leadership role of this new emerging nation fulfilled the covenantal promises of God; God would be their God and they would be His people.

5. DAVID

King David became integral to the future salvation of God's people and the provision of salvation which included an everlasting kingdom (2 Samuel 7:8-17, Psalm 89:28-29). The final fulfillment of the Davidic Covenant will be when Christ returns and we, who have trusted in him, will be in His presence forever.

6. GRACE

God's grace becomes the focus of the new covenant (John 13:34-35, 11 Corinthians 3:6, Hebrews 6:13-20). The covenants of the Old Testament focused on the law. The New Testament reveals the establishment of a different covenant, a new covenant that flows from God's grace. This is a spiritual covenant of God through His son, Jesus Christ, as Redeemer. The new life of a redeemed person comes through faith in Jesus Christ and not by righteous works. It is a powerful gift to those who respond to God's invitation. Hope becomes the "anchor of our souls" (Hebrews 6:19).

When considering small groups in our church ministry, the model of the Old and New Testament covenants create an environment of accountability; an anticipation of promises, and a desire to live righteously. Although what we decide upon in our small group is not a covenant of God in the same sense as the examples just described, when we commit to agree with one another, it is powerful to think that God is interested in and longs to bless our goal and purpose to honor Him.

DESIGNING THE COVENANT

Every group makes a covenant whether they realize it or not. Either it is an assumed covenant (or agreement) or a negotiated covenant. An assumed covenant develops when members have a particular idea of how the group will function during its time together without actually discussing the details. The problem with this process is that most people assume differently. In our negative group experience, my husband and I assumed that the meeting would start and end on time and that we would be participating in the discussion. Unfortunately a designed covenant was not part of this particular group's process and we assumed incorrectly.

The negotiated covenant, on the other hand, is one that has been thoroughly discussed and agreed upon by the participating members. This process minimizes the likelihood of disappointments due to unfulfilled assumptions. A negotiated covenant creates a healthy small group process and should be a top priority in forming a group. Had the first group we attended designed a covenant, the group members would have considered the importance of group participation. Future evaluation would have brought attention to the lack of follow through, misunderstandings, and unfulfilled purposes represented by the group members.

The best process for designing a covenant happens when two or three people commit to creating a small group. With prayer as the foundation, these original organizers should expand to three or four interested people. Precovenanting within this smaller group helps to guide the purposes and goals for the future group. The various reasons for meeting become the purpose of the group and how and when implementation happens become its goals. Purposes can be nebulous, but goals need to be defined, realistic, reachable, and time-oriented. Brainstorm, reshape, talk, reshape, and repeat the process until you feel there is a basic foundation for the particular small group.

As new people indicate an interest in the forming group, you and your team already have determined the initial design. This early work saves much time and effort when discussing the important remaining covenant components with the future group. There are many aspects of the covenant and certainly enough in which the whole group may be involved. Starting out the first night saying, "So what do you want to do, be, study, achieve," sets the group up for frustration, indecision, lack of direction, and potential failure.

For example, let's say one person has a desire to dig deeply into Scripture on a weekly basis. He or she talks to a friend or two and together they become excited and challenged with the privilege of being involved in the leadership of this theoretical group. As the leaders pray about and brainstorm over what this group might look like, particular purposes might be expressed, such as: growing spiritually, building and growing relationships with a small group of people, and accountability to God and each other. Discussions about implementation results in a proposal to meet on Tuesday nights from 7:00 PM to 9:00 PM each week for ten weeks, which the group believes is a defined, realistic, and reachable goal.

As you talk with your friends about forming a small group, be sure to do so in agreement with the person responsible for small groups at your church. Remember to invite twice as many people as you want to see attend and most likely you will end up with your desired group size. Remember to look for diversity (eleven quiet personalities might not produce vibrant discussions). Personal contact is always best; stating that they are not committing to a for-ever meeting, but encourage each one to check it out for one or two weeks before making the final commitment. Advertising in a bulletin or information board alone is usually not productive.

When your first meeting happens, you and your initial team should already have designed a few defining elements of this new small group. The day and time has been established. You promoted the group for the purpose of digging into Scripture, growing spiritually, and creating meaningful relationships. Now you can open up the covenant process by asking a few questions for confirma-tion of the common purposes, or for new ideas. Since the day for the group's meeting has been determined, you might ask: "Is this meeting time best for each of you? Would changing to 6:30 P.M. work better? Should refreshments be available each week?" And, the study material needs to be addressed. Decide in your pre-covenant design on two or three options for study and present them to the group for discussion. Remember not to have your first meeting be all business. Have refreshments, spend time getting to know each other, present a devotional, and have fun!

Now you are on the right track for continuing to design a covenant where each member feels he or she has ownership. They have joined because they know what the group initially is all about. They too are interested in growing spiritually and developing meaningful relationships. With this important foun-dation, the group can continue to shape and reshape the covenant, extending the valuable experience of ownership and belonging.

WHY DESIGN A COVENANT?

Keeping in mind the opening statement of this chapter by Julie Gorman, group beginnings become a foundation and a norm for group life. If we strive for healthy group process, we must articulate the intentions of the group, express hopes and fears, guide the direction and boundaries, outline patterns and norms, provide a structure of accountability and commitment, provide freedom within expectations, and basically shape the group so each person knows what to expect and how to respond. The process may take a few weeks to complete.

Should the covenants be written? Do we have to sign them? These decisions must be part of the covenant process, but generally most groups do not have a signed mandate. A written covenant, however, may be a helpful reminder of the group's purpose and agreements. Of course, adjustments can be made by the group if necessary. Ask for a volunteer to be the scribe in order to record as you design. Have someone reproduce a creative document that can be referred to from time to time. The written covenant becomes a handy tool for important times of evaluation and adjustments when adding or losing members, ending a particular study, or when the group dynamics seem to indicate a problem. If the covenant is not in writing, members will eventually forget the particular commitment they have made and inaccurate assumptions surface once again.

A small group can do virtually anything, but it cannot do and be everything to every member. It is, therefore, important to choose what is in the scope of the group's purpose and what is not. Some groups may prefer more study time and less prayer time or to occasionally deviate and be purely focused on fellowship as the necessity appears. There will be times when you will want to move away from your usual format. Varying your schedule prevents your group from operating in an overly familiar routine. Take time to be fresh and to be creative.

BASIC QUESTIONS TO ASK

Even though some details of the new small group have been previously determined, consider asking these four questions as you start your time together:

1. **Intentions**: Why do you want to be part of this small group?

Finding out why people have chosen to become part of small group reinforces the process of building the covenant. The reasons for joining a small group are myriad. Typically the responses will reflect the desire to be with other people, to build meaningful relationships, to grow spiritually, and sometimes to meet a possible future wife or husband! Finding out people's intentions and recording them becomes the foundation for designing the covenant.

2. Goals and purposes: What do we want to see develop in us as a result of this group?

People join small groups for a variety of reasons. Goals and purposes flow from the intentions expressed. Most purposes will reflect a desire to grow spiritually. Often there is the unspoken cry for being cared for or accepted and included in weekly community where the person feels they will have a sense of belonging. A safe, trusting group of friends is an important foundation for healthy spiritual growth, and this process happens best through mutual commitment to common goals.

3. Expectations: What will make this group worth your time involvement?

Everyone is presented with the responsibility of making good decisions and choices in the face of available opportunities. When making a choice that involves committing a significant segment of time, people want to make sure it is a good investment. Expressing fears and reservations will help them decide if the choice is right for them. For instance, if starting and ending on time is important (and it should be), that issue becomes an important ingredient in the covenant design. If preparation is expected, if members commit to make the group meeting a priority, if the environment is trusting and safe, and shared information is held in strict confidence, then members know what to expect and how to interact.

4. Commitments: What do we want included in our time together?

Small group time together has its limitations. Deciding on a length of time for each meeting helps everyone to decide together what is in and what is out. Options should reflect what the early church modeled in Acts Chapter 2, including fellowship, worship, nurture, mission, and the appropriate time allotment for each of these ingredients. Additional questions to ask or issues to raise might include making group time a priority, the availability of members to one another outside group time, and commitments to outside group social events. All these details are important to discuss in order to maintain healthy expectations for each person involved. Also, having these discussions allows a valuable evaluation process from time to time.

In short, covenants will vary according to the purposes and goals of each group. Groups are formed for particular reasons and interests, allowing them to have their own identity and significance. Looking at the following types of groups, it becomes evident that each group will compose different covenants that serve their purpose. An important reminder: the ingredients of Caring, Growing, and Doing are critical to the health of every group, so be sure to create appropriate space for these aspects of group life according to the group's goals and purposes.

TYPES OF GROUPS

Discipleship groups form with an emphasis on the discipline of Bible study with the goal of spiritual maturity. Often group members form new groups with the desire to train others to do and be the same. Preparation and accountability are expected for this type of group. These groups function best meeting weekly.

Fellowship groups are designed for the purpose of connecting with others in the church family and often have an elder overseeing the meeting. The group focus is generally on friendly gatherings and less on Bible study and accountability. These groups are usually larger than the typical small group, tending to be organized based on geographic proximity and meet less often than discipleship groups. At times they are useful "fishing pools" for developing smaller groups. Due to the size and the process of assignment, geographically-organized fellowship groups often fail to create a caring community. There usually is little cohesive purpose, undeveloped trust levels, and inconsistent attendance. Basically, they are not small groups. Offer them if you must, but call them what they are; an occasional large gathering of people.

Affinity groups focus on similarities of those who attend. While the essential ingredients of group life are included, the group forms around a particular stage of life, gender, activity, common interest, or difficult circumstance. When facilitated in a healthy manner, these groups develop strong trust levels and deep sharing. Most often affinity groups meet weekly or not less than twice a month. Support groups fall into this category.

Nurture groups are similar to the discipleship groups, but often do not include preparation or have the same intensity of study. They can be cross-generational or affinity types and meet weekly or biweekly for varying lengths of time. Many of the popular small groups fall into this category as they provide friendly small gatherings for spiritual growth, care, outreach, and a sense of connection with the larger church community.

Task groups are created for performing particular activities for varying periods of time. The group is organized around a focus of service within the church body or in outreach to the community. A group might form around choirs, ushers, to evaluate areas of evangelism within the various church ministries, or to reach out to those in need with food ministries or job training. Even though the focus is on serving, the three remaining necessary ingredients of small group life (nurture, community, and worship) should be incorporated in the time together.

Spiritual Friendship groups can fall into the "affinity" type but are basically a smaller group of people who yearn to go deeper in their relationship and experience of God. Scripture is central to this type group yet the preparations usually involve reading and reflecting on a particular resource book focusing on a spiritual discipline. The goal here is to understand the importance of establishing reflective rhythms in life and relationship with Christ and one another. High accountability is expected in this type of group which functions best when meeting once a month for the preparation of reading and acting on challenging spiritual formation.

Seeker groups focus on creating a safe environment for those interested in exploring the Christian faith. Great care is taken to ensure that those attending experience a comfortable setting in order for them to freely ask the difficult questions about life and faith, as well as to express their own doubts and fears. These groups most often meet weekly. Creating effective fellowship for building relationships is critical for establishing an environment of comfort and safety of these groups.

INGREDIENTS OF SMALL GROUP LIFE

If you consider the following diagrams as the time represented in your small group meeting, each component needs to have a time value allotted to it. For instance, if you were in a nurture group, you would plan to spend significant time reading and studying the Bible. In a prayer group, a larger portion of the time would be spent in prayer. If you are a task group, most of your time will be attributed to performing the task. If you consider the importance of all four ingredients, the challenge is designating appropriate time segments of your meeting to each ingredient.

Using the task group as an example, the challenge is to find the moments to start with a short devotional and prayer before setting out to accomplish the task. Fellowship happens naturally throughout the interaction members have with one another while doing the task. Alternatively, if the group's purpose is fellowship, a wise leader would challenge the group to include worship and a short study while not forgetting those opportunities to serve those in need.

INGREDIENT SEGMENTS OF SMALL GROUP MEETINGS

FOUR NECESSARY INGREDIENTS

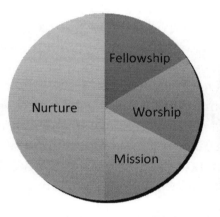

NURTURE GROUP

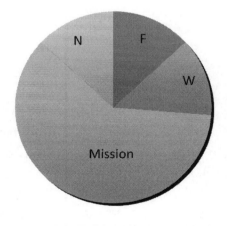

MISSION OR TASK GROUP

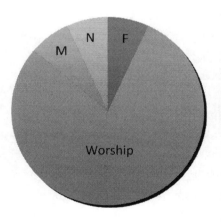

PRAYER GROUP

Consider the circle representative of how you spend time in your small group meetings. According to the type of group you are, each segment is allotted a specific time allotment. This becomes a guide for moving your group through the essential ingredients of small group life and honors the covenant commitment the group has designed together.

Although mission is a very important ingredient in the life of a small group, realistically mission will not happen each week unless that is the purpose and focus of the group. For example, having a small group work in a city soup kitchen is a significant act of compassion and mission. However, this activity most likely would not happen frequently, but should be considered (or something similar) when the group is in the design process. The small group needs to be challenged with incorporating the vital ingredient of mission into the covenant. On the other hand, mission, in caring for tangible needs within the church family, can be more easily implemented and exercised more often.

Remember rigid flexibility! This is not military school and we don't crack the whip at each meeting in order to keep strict timing. The process outlined above exists to help you think through the important aspects of group life. It is always helpful to sketch out a circle of time as you begin to design a group. Consider the value of creativity, and vary the order of the various components of group life. Make it fresh and stimulating and try to keep on schedule!

NEXT STEPS IN EARLY GROUP FORMATION

In addition to the particulars of the covenant goals and purposes, there are important additional decisions the group needs to make:

I. STUDY MATERIAL

With a group forming for the first time, it is a disadvantage to begin the first night asking: "What do you want to study?" Immediately you are inviting twelve different opinions. The best process is to have three or four study guides with you to present to the new group for consideration. As previously mentioned, groups should start with the subject or focus predetermined. Having established the purpose of the group, people are drawn to join through mutual interest. When starting a group, an eight-week study works well. It is long enough for bonding to begin, but short enough to evaluate and redesign the group if needed. If you choose a longer study for the next stage of your group life, you are building further commitment into the group. Clarifying the starting and ending point of a group study allows the freedom for someone to drop out at the end of a particular study and move on to another option without feeling awkward.

2. PREPARATION

Now that you have decided what type of group you will be and the goals and purposes are defined, there are other important issues to discuss. As you designate appropriate time segments to group activities according to your goals, you must reach agreement on expectations. For example, if you plan forty-five minutes to do Bible study, make sure you are in agreement on whether or not preparation is expected. Many resources will tell you that one way to kill a group is to require preparation. If a group forms around the model of discipleship, preparation is part of the process. What kills a group is not having an agreement as to what is expected. On the other hand, your group may be a nurture group where Scripture is studied in the context of the group meeting and not through prior personal preparation. Remember, if you have chosen a particular guidebook and no preparation is expected, the leader is the only one who needs the guidebook.

3. LEADERSHIP ROLES

As the leader, you will lead the new group through the first few weeks. This contributes to creating a safe environment as group members expect to have an assigned leader. Ideally, you will have an apprentice or co-leader as part of the team, but often this person is discovered as the group grows together. You might suggest the idea of a co-leader further into your time together if it becomes apparent that sharing some of the group facilitation would utilize individual spiritual gifts that are revealed in other members. Remember, small groups are perfect venues for leadership development. However, for the duration of the small group, there must be a designated leader ultimately responsible for evaluation, troubleshooting, and for the accountability to the small group ministry of your church. Leadership of a small group does not rotate, but the role of discussion facilitator may.

4. MEETING ENVIRONMENT

How often will you meet? Where will you gather? Deciding the frequency of your times together is important. If the expectations are negotiable, you should consider the value in meeting weekly. Initially, the weekly meeting helps to bond the group faster. After finishing one study, you might evaluate and change to every other week. However, most people who experience healthy, meaningful small groups anticipate the interaction on a weekly basis. Meeting every other week tends to weaken effective group development, especially if a person misses one meeting resulting in only monthly attendance. Think about your stated goals and purposes in making the decision about meeting frequency. Along with that you will need to decide whether to rotate the meeting place and what other protocols will be followed. For example, what is the group's view about allowing children, beepers, cell phones, animals, and other distractions. The environment is important.

Take time to think about and list the impediments. For instance, couples with young children find it difficult to attend small groups due to babysitting barriers. As a caring group, you might want to brainstorm about creative ways of involving these children for part of the meeting, or provide babysitting somewhere else. Perhaps the group could contribute toward the babysitting fee if just one or two couples in the group have children. Just make sure everyone is in agreement.

5. OPEN OR CLOSED

A major decision for your group is to decide whether your group will be open to new people each week or limited to those who first signed up. There are pros and cons for each decision. It is true that a group will bond faster and trust levels will deepen more quickly when the same people meet week after week. When you open up the group to new people too often, trust levels are harder to create and deep sharing is more difficult. Therefore, an early decision on how new members may be admitted and how large the group can become should be addressed. While most groups do not like to think about multiplying, those that continually increase in numbers should keep in mind that having a group larger than twelve is a barrier for effective discussion, for establishing high trust levels, and for developing effective caring relationships. A design for breaking into smaller groups within this large, growing group needs to be established.

On the other hand, there definitely are advantages to group growth. Adding new people is a constant opportunity for people to be cared for and connected in church life. Open groups denounce that small groups are cliques. It stretches members in their acceptance of others and willingness to be flexible. But, given the difficulties that growth may present, make sure this decision is clear in the minds of all the members. Being open for the first two weeks and closed for the remaining six is a good compromise. If your group is visibly listed, you might use a different wording such as at capacity or full to send a friendlier message. Opening up again at the end of a study allows people to leave if they feel it is necessary and it presents an opportunity to bring in new people. It's a significant dynamic so make sure everyone is in agreement.

6. MULTIPLYING

Being committed to multiplying your group is a challenging but rewarding focus. It expands the small group ministry of your church and allows more people to experience the transforming life you have experienced. For example, at one of my training seminars, I challenged a group leader who was reluctant to confront his group with this important mindset. He knew it would not go over well. A while later he responded:

> "I don't know if I told you this or not, but I am taking your advice about not closing our group. We added three new couples and it is working wonderfully. If we get too big, then we'll just have to split, but for now, it's great. It's easy to stay the same and be more comfortable. So glad for the advice!"

Another example is one I love to share. At our city church there are over thirty small groups designed especially for connecting weekly those in their twenties. This ministry started from one small group, all of whom were potential, dynamite leaders. Avoiding me at all cost, they functioned as a tight group of close friends and were not receptive to my multiply your group challenge! In time they took initial steps of multiplication and God blessed their willingness, first with three new groups, then fifteen, and now over thirty. Their vision for their peer group resulted in over four hundred young men and women participating in significant healthy spiritual community.

In a large church it becomes even more critical to have caring venues in place if you want young people to stay. It's too easy to come to weekend worship and slip out unnoticed. Remember, young people are searching for meaningful relationships and role models. As leaders we need to keep in mind the knowing, loving, serving, admonishing, and celebrating aspects of small group life in order for life-change and renewal to become a reality in the lives of each individual.

UNDERSTANDING PERSONAL COMMITMENT

With the details in place for the selected study, what to include in group meetings, where to meet, starting and ending time, how and when new people may join, and other details of how the group will function, it is equally import-ant to make decisions concerning the expectations of those committed to the process of forming this new group. To that end, the following five aspects of healthy small group process need to be discussed and woven into the group's covenant commitment.

1. ATTENDANCE

The priority of attendance should be stressed. Telling people that their presence is important to the life of the group helps because it is true. What will it take to have people excited about attending the group? When asked to attend a function on the night of their small group meeting, will they choose their group or another option? Stressing the importance of life together and growing spiritually encourages a commitment from the members to attend. Do all you can to encourage members to make the group meetings a priority. Calling or emailing when someone has missed a meeting works well to encour-age attendance. You should emphasize what happened in the group and how they were missed rather than an accusatory comment of "Where were you?"

2. PARTICIPATION

Encourage members to enter into the discussion and sharing. Everyone's contribution is important. It is here that, through a bit of humor, you can warn people about dominating a discussion or being comfortable just listening to others. Key to this process is acquiring the ability to ask good questions through creative communication skills. (The topics concerning effective discussion and different personality roles will be addressed more fully in Chapter Seven.) If your group is too large, the quiet person remains comfortably quiet and the dominant person continues to dominate. Therefore, remind and encourage members often to participate appropriately.

3. CONFIDENTIALITY

Agreeing not to repeat conversations and stories that are shared within the group context is critical to the safety and honesty of the group. When a certain level of trust is developed, self-disclosure begins to happen. Significant spiritual growth can occur when members feel that they can trust other group members, share difficult circumstances, and experience the challenge of applying truth to personal situations while being held accountable. If a member learns that his or her vulnerability in revealing life stories ends up as a topic for Wednesday night's prayer meeting, trust is destroyed. Unless the person has given permission for information to be shared with others, sharing information outside the group that is meant to stay within results in nothing more than gossip. A strong commitment to confidentiality is a significant component of a group's covenant.

4. RESPECT AND CARE

It is wise to remind group members to refrain from judging one another, giving advice (unless asked for), or criticizing the actions of another member. Again the goal is to create a healthy, safe place for the issues of life to be discussed and responded to through the study of Scripture. The group must be sensitive to the needs of others, assist when appropriate, but most importantly, take the time to listen with loving acceptance regardless of life situations. And, when trust levels develop, accountability has its place. This all happens in due time and when the leader gently facilitates the group through the various stages of growth.

Covenants build as your group bonds and the trust level rises. At your first meeting, discuss the essentials for getting off to a good start and over the next meeting or two, evaluate and add decisions as time and circumstances permit. Remember to start your delegation process by asking someone to write down the details of your decisions. This will allow the group to see clearly what they have committed to and will get your group off to a solid start.

EVALUATION IS KEY TO HEALTHY GROUPS

It is essential to evaluate what is working well in the group and what is not. From time to time, look over your covenant and see where improvements may be made. Basic questions might include: "What is working well?" or "What changes should we make and why?" Certain times are better than others for purposes of revisiting your covenant as your group life develops:

1. **At regular intervals** helps your group to stay focused on the goals and purposes of your time together. As you grow as a caring community, these purposes may change. If you have a written covenant, you can discuss what is working and what is not. By making appropriate changes, your group life is improved and becomes healthier. By revisiting the covenant at regular intervals, small group life becomes extended and not static or stale as changes often are made and new items added. Make it a habit to revisit your covenant at the end of each designated study guide.

2. **When a new person joins**, he or she needs to know what the group is all about. Perhaps this new member has joined purely because he or she is attracted to your goals and purposes. Often, however, small group ministries have the responsibility of putting new people into groups, and potential members are placed according to their schedule for the right night or preferred mix of people. (Unfortunately groups formed in this procedure seem to experience high attrition.) In this case, it is critical that the new person, who was not involved in the original covenant making, becomes familiar with the defining agreements of the group covenant. By expressing the purposes and goals, and what has been decided about the meeting content, the new person becomes aware of the group expectations and adjusts accordingly. Now the new member has the opportunity to know what to expect, rather than defaulting to an assumed covenant.

Also, keep in mind that it is far more comfortable for the new person if they are not the only one added. Joining a group while not knowing the group history or experiences can become uncomfortable and isolating when old stories are told and jokes remembered. If possible, consider adding more than one person at a time when you open the group to new members.

3. **When a person leaves** there is obviously a reason. Unhealthy groups often are not aware of the reason why a member leaves and tend to shrug it off. It is important, therefore, to review your covenant when someone leaves, particularly if you know the member has felt that the group did not meet his or her expectations. This also becomes a time when decisions for bringing in new people may be discussed. People leave for a variety of reasons, including starting late, ending late, agreeing to prepare and not getting to the discussion,

personalities that are difficult and not handled well by the leader, lack of prayer or worship, and subject matter that is not of interest to them.

4. **When a crisis happens in your group**, evaluate the situation and see how the crisis might have been averted. Did it have anything to do with the covenant understanding, or lack thereof? If the crisis was due to conflict, do you know the process of resolution? Again, difficult personalities such as the one who dominates, the one who thinks they are the theological expert, or the one who constantly disagrees with ideas contrary to theirs, cause much anxiety and create an unhealthy group environment. These personalities will be discussed more fully in Chapter Eight.

COVENANTS: A TEMPLATE TO FOLLOW

It is easy to see that a group has potential to fail when key aspects of group life are not discussed and common ground reached. Consider the following example of some small group covenant ideas you might use as a template for creating your own group covenant. Be creative and delegate the final document to someone in the group who has design skills. Have members tuck away a copy in their Bibles as a personal reminder and for future reference. Your small group does not want to reflect a list of rules and regulations, but provide guidelines for creating a healthy group environment for life transformation.

The Awesome Group!

Purposes

- To get to know God in a more personal way
- To understand what we believe as Christians
- To connect with other believers
- To belong to a small group that will support me in my spiritual growth
- To genuinely show care in tangible ways
- To have fun!

Goals

- Allow 20 minutes for sharing and unpacking our stories
- Allow 40 minutes for Bible study
- Allow 30 minutes for prayer
- Plan two outreach events/year together
- Plan social times outside regular meetings once/quarter such as celebrating birthdays or holidays

Length, Times and Locations of Meetings

Length: 7-8:30 pm and we will start and end on time!
Day: Monday evenings for eight weeks
Location: Meet at the home of the designated leader or host

Significant Agreements

Priority: We will make our small group a priority over other activities.
Participation: We will prepare the lesson prior to each meeting.
Confidentiality: What is shared in our small group stays in our small group.
Open Group: We will open our group at the end of each short study.
Support: We will be willing to give care and support at all times.
Accountability: We will strive for truth telling and responsibility for our behavior.

Reminder: Do your best to lead your group through a well-prepared format for the evening. But keep in mind, occasionally there are times when you need to let the Holy Spirit intervene and change the course. This is when you willingly discard your prepared plans in order to care for a member with a serious need. The following experience was a perfect example to me concerning the power of the Holy Spirit in creating moments where love, care, and attention became more important than the powerful (so I thought) lesson I had prepared.

One Sunday night I was leading a membership class of ten people. It was our fourth time together and we were to discuss the role of the Holy Spirit throughout Scripture and in our lives. I thought I was fairly creative in preparing a lesson where I had traced many excellent verses describing the presence and acts of the Holy Spirit through the Old and New Testaments. I handed out several verses to each person and we began reading each verse without making comments. The content was building with great power when I noticed one young lady being distracted by the woman sitting next to me. Then I became distracted. The woman next to me was grabbing her neck and rubbing her chest. "Ruth, what is wrong?" I commented (perhaps with a bit of annoyance). Her response was that she was experiencing a similar pain to her previous heart attack episode.

With this disturbing development, we jumped up, gathered around her, prayed for her while someone went to get a car. We should have called 911, but a major hospital was three blocks away. Three people escorted her to the hospital and stayed with her until after her examination and the arrival of her close friend.

While it certainly was an example of a caring small group, I admit that I was initially very disappointed that my creative small group lesson was all for naught since we had to keep on a weekly schedule. It also was a reminder to me of the results of an earlier spiritual gift assessment I had taken, in which I was diagnosed as having less compassion than perhaps I should. I had been working on developing in this area for some time. Was my experience an indication that I was not making headway? Fortunately the woman was fine a couple of days later and evidently had reacted adversely to a new prescription. I called her each day and soon she was back participating in the group. Sometimes the prepared lessons that you think are quite powerful get tossed aside for a more important issue, but hopefully not every week. Again, a useful characteristic for a small group leader is to have rigid flexibility.

The importance of covenant building in small group life cannot be overstated. It must be understood and experienced. Proper covenant building makes or breaks the success of a small group. Many people cringe when approached with the process of covenant building as they feel it is too legalistic. So take care not construct the covenant to look like a list of rules and regulations. Covenants held a significant role in the emerging Christian church and we continue to exist under the loving new covenant of grace that God so lavishly pours down upon us. Covenants do not have to be signed in blood. Instead, when creatively designed, they have significant use for evaluating and improving a group's accountability and vision. Don't forget, a group will always have a covenant. The question is whether it will be unstated and assumed by individuals; or openly discussed and negotiated by the group.

So, ask the question again: Why covenants? Covenants influence the health of a small group in strategic ways. Once everyone knows what is in and what is out, what expectations and boundaries are in place, members start to share their lives knowing that there are a group of people in agreement on vision and process. When members see their friends praying for them, caring for their lives spiritually and physically, they feel connected to the larger community that listens to them while taking the time to respond for their good. It is at this moment that each member experiences the reality that God takes ordinary people and makes them into extraordinary people by the power of His Spirit. This is Scripture coming alive; "speaking the truth in love" (Ephesians 4:15).

The healthy small group becomes that strategic place for loving, knowing, serving, admonishing, and celebrating one another as lives are transformed and churches renewed. It is here that we dare to allow God into the unexplored or unknown areas of our life because we have a trusted group of like-minded pilgrims with whom we share the journey. It is at this point when we can express our need for people to listen, pray, and commit to growing together during the good experiences and the difficult situations of life. This process naturally leads to great worship. In the next chapter, we will explore creative ways to bring fresh and exciting ideas of worship into group life that allows everyone to participate.

Please prepare the following Bible study for your next group gathering. Be thinking about ways to encourage your future group and the steps you will take to introduce the importance of designing a covenant.

AGREEING TO AGREE

1. TELL

- » Can you think of a time when you confided in a group only to have the news spread outside your group? Briefly describe your emotions and reactions.
- » Have you participated in a group that included an agreement or covenant? If so, what personal value did the covenant bring to your group experience? In what way did the covenant make you feel more comfortable with the group expectations?
- » If you were to design a covenant for the small group training group you are presently involved, what might be some of the important components to include?

2. DISCUSS

Think about and discuss how some of the ideas and illustrations presented in this chapter might help improve the health of your group or assist you, perhaps for the first time, in forming a new small group. Briefly discuss one example of a positive and a negative experience with small group life you have experienced. Define the lack of or the inclusion of the variables that made them positive or negative.

A LIFE CHANGING PROPHECY

Read Jeremiah 31:33-34

3. SCRIPTURE

For your preparation this week, take extra time to read a few Scriptures focused on covenants: Genesis 9:8-17; Genesis 15:9-20,17; 2 Samuel 7:5-16. In these passages we see a picture of God making promises with specific individuals and groups of people. They include promises of land, continued priesthood, continued relationship with God, and the promise of a future Savior for God's people through the line of David. What do you learn about the particulars of these old covenants? What were the limitations?

Read the portion of Jeremiah identified above. Jeremiah wrote this passage while confined in the court of the guard. The words have tremendous influence on the New Testament doctrine. It is a commonly held view that the concept of the new covenant is Jeremiah's greatest contribution to biblical truth concerning messianic times. For some additional reading, turn to Hebrews 8:5-6; 9:3-15, and 1 Corinthians 11:24-25.

Look (observation)

» What was the new covenant described by Jeremiah? In what way does this new covenant differ from the old?
» What is the stated future promise?
» What are some characteristics of God we observe from these verses?

Think (interpretation)

» What does Jeremiah imply to his readers through this Scripture?
» What is significant about the differences with the old and the new covenant that would be meaningful and encouraging to Jeremiah's readers?

Act (application)

» Does this promise from Scripture apply to you? If so, how and why?
» We all experience people breaking promises with us and we with them. Describe your heart-felt response towards God and His faithful covenant knowing His covenant of grace will not be broken.
» Think of a circumstance in your life where it helps to know that God is a God of compassion. In what way can you begin to improve your response to His love and forgiveness?
» Think about how you could be more open for God to put His Word in your mind and write it on your heart? What would that look like?
» Consider the subject of covenants concerning small group process. In what way will designing a covenant improve your present group or assist in getting you off to a great start with a new group?

4. PRAYER

Pray with and for one another. Pray for your future groups and for God's wise leading as you prepare for your initial gatherings.

5. PREPARATION

Through this new covenant, the death and resurrection of Jesus Christ, we have entered into a new relationship with God. Because of the new covenant's fulfillment, our personal decision to be identified with Jesus Christ is the most precious gift we will ever receive. Coming together as a healthy small group becomes a place to care for and connect with one another and to provide a safe place for the Holy Spirit to change lives. This caring environment is also an opportunity to worship a living God and celebrate our position as his children. We too, as a community of believers, must take opportunities to praise God through song, prayer, and other expressions.

Our next chapter will include many helpful ideas in creating a time of worship that will be exciting and productive in your spiritual journey. Select a discussion leader for the next session and during the week read the next chapter on worship. Prepare the Bible study.

"May the God of peace,
who through the blood of the eternal covenant
brought back from the dead our Lord Jesus,
that great Shepherd of the sheep, equip you with
everything good for doing his will,
and may he work in us what is pleasing to him
through Jesus Christ, to whom be glory
for ever and ever. Amen."

Hebrews 13:20

WORSHIP:
FOCUSING ON GOD

"Worship does not satisfy our hunger for God—it whets our appetite. Our need of God is not taken care of by engaging in worship—it deepens."

Eugene Peterson, *A Long Obedience in the Same Direction*

Have you ever had one of those uniquely exciting, fulfilling, Spirit-filled experiences of corporate worship? What was it about that worship time that stands out in your mind? Gathering together in Jesus' name, singing praises, expressing thanksgiving, requesting His will, and being united in purpose leaves each of us with an awesome encounter with God.

I remember attending an InterVarsity conference where I first learned the song "Shout to the Lord." The impact was huge and now years later when I hear the chorus, I remember all my surroundings and the powerful experience of the weekend. At an Alpha Course Training Conference[39], I experienced singing in

---

39 The Alpha Course is a ten week introduction to the Christian faith. Emphasis is placed on creating a safe place where people can ask the difficult questions of life. Resources can be found at selected Christian bookstores or http.//www.alphausa.org.

the Spirit where a crowd of 500 people hummed one note in perfect unison. Being a musician and having worked with choirs, I know how difficult singing in perfect unison can be. I was most amazed at the true pitch and the beauty of the spontaneous sound. Participating in congregational hymn singing, large or small, makes my soul soar with love to the Lord, for who He is and what He has done. Unfortunately most small groups do not include this essential ingredient of worship in the life of their meetings. Worship, whatever shape or form, is a component that must not be overlooked or short-changed.

God calls believers to worship. After Jesus had ministered to the woman at the well, he declared that worship was taking on a new approach from what the tradition of that time practiced: "Yet a time is coming and has now come when the true worshipers will worship the Father in spirit and truth, for they are the kind of worshipers the Father seeks" (John 4:23). We have those opportunities in the small group setting and we often neglect the privilege of that freedom. God is seeking us and we respond to Him in worship. "Singing, praying, praising all may lead to worship, but worship is more than any of them. Our spirit must be ignited by the divine fire."[40] Richard Foster reminds us that God longs to spend time with us and is seeking us to worship and glorify Him.

There are many ways to worship God in small groups. Often people confine the term to having a time of prayer at the beginning or end of the group meeting, but in fact there are several meaningful ways to engage your group in worship beyond prayer. Praise, thanksgiving, music, Scripture reading, spiritual disciplines of reflection, meditation, personal psalms and prayers, spiritual autobiographies, and silence ought to be included from time to time.

PURPOSE OF WORSHIP

The key issue in worship is to turn our thoughts and attention totally to God. It is a time of being honest in praise and vulnerable in confession. It becomes a time for letting God know how much we love and adore Him for who He is and what He has done. Worship is an integral part of group process. It also presents an opportunity to delegate the worship segment of your group time to someone gifted in this area. Often the lack of worship stems from the leaders inability to be creative or interest in preparing some aspect of group life that is unfamiliar to him or her. Here's a wonderful opportunity

---

40 Richard J. Foster, The Celebration of Discipline (San Francisco: Harper, 1988), 159. Foster has written many resources for understanding and practicing the spiritual disciplines.

to discover and utilize spiritual and natural gifts of group members and assign them a leadership role.

PSALMS

The Psalms were written as prayers and often sung. People of God have used the Psalms for thousands of years in seeking guidance, solace, and wisdom concerning daily life experiences. Using the Psalms as preparation to meet God or as a response to His Word can be quite powerful. Each Psalm reveals the intimate thoughts, cares, and desires of its author. Through them, we can experience honest praise, concern, anxiety, anger, thanksgiving, and the longing for and assurance of God's presence. Take time to include the Psalms in your worship time. Meditate and reflect on repeated words, or focus on one word that paints a powerful picture of God.

Some of us tend to read the well-known psalms quickly and superficially because we have heard them for years. While reading Psalm 46:1-2, the fact that "God is our refuge and strength, an ever-present help in trouble and therefore we will not fear," we know well. However, when we ponder those words, we have to admit that often we don't rely on God for our strength. We try to do things in our own strength. And when we are in trouble, we wonder where God is and are often filled with fear. To reflect upon and understand the power of each word causes each of us to realize that knowing Psalm 46 intellectually is very different from living Psalm 46 with confidence of Who God is and His protective love for us.

Be creative and recite the Psalms responsively within the group. Vary your translations. Reading from a paraphrase like The Message[41] often puts unfamiliar vernacular into the more contemporary, allowing the possibility of a better understanding and discussion. Using the Psalms in worship creates meaningful praise, prayer, and identification with emotions and experiences expressed by the psalmists.

When I first became familiar with Scripture and in particular the Psalms, I wondered who Selah was since she was mentioned so often in the King James version I read. Learning later that Selah was a request for pause and reflection,

---

41 Eugene Peterson, The Message (Colorado Springs, Colorado: NavPress, 1994). This paraphrase of Scripture is helpful for understanding Scripture in relevant, contemporary expression.

I came to understand the importance of the verse and the intention of its message in a clearer way. Many of the liturgical churches model the pause for reflection, the Selah, and it allows the worshippers to participate in acknowledging the message, correction, or affirmation that is implied in the text.

Be creative instead of getting into a routine. Try reading the Psalms in your group, making those intended pauses once in a while as doing so enhances the worship style. Reading a psalm prepares each heart and soul for your time together. Celebrate God by sharing a favorite psalm and its impact on your life, or by sharing a personally written psalm as a response to God and His loving watchful care.

> "There is one thing still remaining which cannot be neglected without great injury to your devotions: to begin all your prayers with a psalm. There is nothing that so clears a way for your prayers; nothing that so disperses dullness of heart; nothing that so purifies the soul from poor and little passions; nothing that so opens heaven or carries your sense of delight in God; they awaken holy desires; they teach how to ask, and they prevail with God to give. They kindle a holy flame; they turn your heart into an altar; they turn your prayers into incense, and carry them as sweet-smelling savor to the throne of grace." (William Law: A Serious Call to a Devout and Holy Life)

PRAYER

Prayer is one of the basic spiritual disciplines. As William Carey has written, "Prayer – secret, fervent, believing prayer – lies at the root of all personal godliness."[42]

Without a consistent and significant prayer life, a Christian's life is void of power and knowledge about God. Prayer is communicating with God. It is a necessity for living the abundant life and the means of coming to know God more intimately. Prayer becomes the barometer of our spirituality. In a group of Christians who are committed to spiritual growth and mutual support, prayer is a major key to experiencing the presence and intervention of God in our individual lives. Unfortunately, we sometimes make unwise choices with our priorities and neglect times of personal prayer. Therefore, the small group arena can be a

---

42 William Carey quoted in E. M. Bounds, Power Through Prayer, (Chicago, Illinois: Moody Press), 23.

powerful venue for helping people experience healthy and significant methods of prayer that encourage them in their personal interaction with God.

PRAYER REMINDERS

There are important reasons why we pray. Be reminded and encouraged by the following:

1. Our Lord has asked us – even commanded us – to pray without ceasing.
2. Our Lord invites us to fellowship with Him, to enjoy intimate, deep communion.
3. Prayer helps transport us from our own agenda to God's agenda, from our will to His.
4. It helps us grow in our relationship to God.
5. It allows us to be used by God to advance His work.
6. God delights in answering our prayers.
7. It provides the spiritual power we need, power that can come only from God.
8. Prayer and the Word are the means by which to defeat the enemy Satan and to live victoriously.
9. There is no higher privilege in life than to communicate with the living God, the Creator and Sustainer of all.
10. Prayer ushers us into the very presence of God![43]

CONSIDER THESE VERSES

- » And when you pray (Matthew 6:5)
- » But when you pray (Matthew 6:6)
- » This is how you should pray (Matthew 6:9)
- » Ask, seek, knock (Luke 11:9)
- » Devote yourselves to prayer (Colossians 4:2)
- » Pray continually (1 Thessalonians 5:17)

At the beginning of every new small group, prayer needs to be carefully developed and nurtured. Use the list above to remind people or perhaps inform them for the first time about the essence and value of prayer. Often when

---

43 Paul Cedar, A Life of Prayer (Nashville, Tennessee: Word, 1998), 33-34.

approaching the beginning stages of developing the covenant and when the question about hopes and fears is addressed, you might find more than one person verbalizing the fear of having to pray aloud. If it isn't expressed, most likely someone in the group is anxious and stressed over the possibility. So, approach prayer carefully, and begin by modeling.

As you start your time together, open in a simple prayer and close your time together with a short prayer as well. In the subsequent meetings you can extend the opportunity to anyone who might like to say a one or two sentence prayer. Involve your group, create the excitement of prayer, and develop the comfort level allowing each one the privilege of participating. In leading a group of young believers, you might start your nurture component with a study on prayer.

BARRIERS FOR EFFECTIVE PRAYER

Prayer honors God, yet in our small group meetings, we often leave the privilege of praying to the last minute. Sometimes prayer never happens. If there is time for prayer, people take their turn and quietly express love, praise, thanksgiving, and their concerns in an honest and open way. But sometimes there are patterns that develop that discourage or inhibit the prayer experience of those in the group.

When asked what a frequent obstacle or barrier to having meaningful prayer might be, the response most always reflects the length of time taken to share prayer requests. Suddenly there are only five minutes or so left to pray! If we agree that prayer lies at the root of all personal godliness and that God delights in our prayers, we have certainly short-changed the small group members of not only the power of prayer, but also the privilege of prayer when we don't leave time to pray. Remembering the word briefly is helpful in frequent situations. If you ask that each prayer request be presented briefly and remind them that God knows all the details, you help the process along. Perhaps you could model with a prayer request of your own.

Often it is helpful to go into the prayer time without verbalizing the request to the group, but presenting the request, through prayer, before God. This approach curtails the length and details of the requests. You do have to keep in mind, however, in the early stages of group life, it is a valuable time to listen to a few details of a prayer concern in order to encourage self-disclosure. The wise action, following initial expression, would be to discourage repeating all the details on a weekly basis and move more quickly into the prayer time.

Another source of frustration with the prayer segment happens with valiant prayer warriors who are part of the group and who often dominate. Prayer warriors are critical to the Christian faith but unfortunately, in small group process, they often believe it is up to them to pray for everybody and everything mentioned. It is hard to find fault with this energetic need to pray so inclusively, however, it becomes discouraging to many in a group when the prayer time is monopolized by one or two people. It is difficult to correct a person so excited about praying, yet in this scenario, our minds wander as we try to think of what might be left for us to pray. This is hardly praying in one accord.

When the group covenant is formed, a segment of time needs to be allotted for prayer. It is a challenge at times to have everyone in the group eager to participate in prayer. A safe, trusting, and comfortable environment needs to be created for those who are learning to pray for the first time or who might be shy about praying aloud.

GUIDELINES FOR HEALTHY PRAYER TIMES

A few general reminders concerning safe environment for prayer are important to remember; caution should be exercised in a couple of ways. It is preferable not to go around the circle when you are praying. Secondly, in the early stage of your group, you should not call on anyone to pray unless you have it prearranged. You cannot expect that everyone knows how to pray or wants to pray aloud. There are other good reasons as well for these cautions, and perhaps I am a bit sensitive, but consider the following experience.

As a new believer, I found myself sitting in a circle of fifteen or so people. We had previously heard a missionary speak at our mission conference. The leader of the group announced that we would begin our prayer time and go around the circle to her left. I was sitting across from her in the circle. Do you have any idea how a new believer who does not know how to pray let alone pray aloud feels in a situation like that? The prayer started. My heart was beating stronger and stronger with my nervousness. I finally thought of something I could say and suddenly someone else said it. It became my turn. I said something like "Thank you for all the Bibles in Russia" and was silent. I don't think Russia was the topic of the evening.

After the meeting, I transferred my experience of panic upon my date (who would later become my husband) blaming him for the stressful situation I experienced (unfair blame and totally not his fault). Had I not been gently encouraged by him at that moment, I might never have wanted to attend a group like that again. To this day I try to break the pattern of going around the circle when praying in a group.

When we learn to offer up different sacrifices of praise in unified prayer, the small group experience of worship can become a powerful impact on each member. Often it is in the small group that prayer takes root and becomes a way of life. The following methods of prayer are some examples you might want to incorporate in your group time. They all have value and reflect various stages of trust and spiritual growth of each person. Be aware of the dynamics and strive to utilize a format that will help members be comfortable in participating. It will depend upon their level of spiritual maturity and willingness.

ACTS: This popular format is useful for allowing everyone to participate in the prayer process. The person who is leading prayer for the evening starts each component. Through this format, everyone is focused on one subject of the prayer. Again, it is important when introducing this method to give everyone the option to pray or not to pray, and encourage people to use short sentence prayers such as the conversational prayer. Another valuable guideline is to make clear that everyone may enter into verbal prayer more than once, or not at all.

1. **A** becomes the time for adoration. We praise God for Who He Is. This might include saying audibly the Names of God, listing His Attributes, or reading a Psalm. This becomes an effective way for those who are new to prayer to participate as it might involve just one word. Psalm 145 is one of the many psalms that express praise and adoration: "I will exalt you, my God the King; I will praise your name for ever and ever" (Psalm 145:1).

2. **C** introduces the small group to the opportunity for open confession. God calls us to confession, repentance, and the blessing of forgiveness. As believers, we are to recognize and grieve over our sins. Initially it is best to ask for silence during the confession. At some point we might suggest confession in the form of silence or, if people feel comfortable, audible. What a thrill to hear group members cry out to God for forgiveness. The leader can model this in a sensitive appropriate manner. Reminding members that if we confess our sins, God in His grace, forgives and restores us to righteousness (1 John 1:9). Use

Psalm 51:1-4 or take an opportunity to use the paraphrase such as The Message and have group members quietly respond.

> Generous in love—God, give grace!
>   huge in mercy—wipe out my bad record.
> Scrub away my guilt,
>   soak out my sins in your laundry.
> I know how bad I've been;
>   my sins are staring me down.
> You're the one I've violated, and you've seen
>   it all, seen the full extent of my evil.
> You have all the facts before you;
>   whatever you decide about me is fair.[44] (Psalm 51:1-4)

Whatever you choose to include, it is important to create a safe place for people to experience the Holy Spirit in the life-changing process. Make it comfortable at first and in time intentionally stretch and move the members into more self-disclosure and risk. It takes spiritual discernment to do this effectively.

3. **T** gives opportunity for thanking God for what He has done. Recall answers to prayers, express the privilege of being a child of God, thank Him for the privilege of being called into service, and basically all facets of life. This might also include suffering and grief. We need to recognize that God is sovereign and in control and therefore thank Him for His presence during a difficult time. For example, Psalm 107 reflects thanksgiving and praise: "Give thanks to the Lord, for he is good; his love endures forever" (Psalm 107:1).

4. **S** becomes the supplication part of our prayer. Perhaps the requests are verbal and certainly some will be unspoken. We have prepared our soul for asking and receiving through the adoration, confession, and thanksgiving. In confidence, we ask in His will. Begin this part of prayer with a verse such as Mark 11:24: "I tell you, whatever you ask for in prayer, believe that you have received it and it will be yours." Entering a time of prayer with confidence is powerful.

During this time of supplication, we pray for ourselves with personal requests and we pray intercessory prayer for our friends and family. Initially it is wise to suggest that prayer requests be for personal concerns or perhaps the immediate

---

44 Peterson, 722.

family. This allows each member to become sensitive and caring in the process of self-disclosure, the getting to know you aspect of small group life.

When prayer requests reach out to the needs of various friends or acquaintances, attention is diverted from personal issues and the process of accountability with one another develops at a slower pace. Often it is more comfortable to ask for prayer for a friend than disclose a personal need, so think about your covenant and how you agreed to spend your time in prayer. Focusing on friends, church, ministries, and leaders of our country certainly should be included, but don't let these issues override the importance of personal needs and care for the group members.

Conversational prayer is an excellent tool for encouraging everyone to participate. It is here that the new believer or the quiet personality can cultivate confidence in praying aloud. By writing down all brief prayer requests, the prayer leader can introduce each concern and let the group as a whole pray for that particular issue. (And, remember do not go around the circle!). This creates a sense of praying together in unity as each person is not thinking about what has not been prayed for, rather in what way they might add their agreement. The leader needs to stress that the pattern is sentence prayers allowing each person to pray as often as they wish.

The goal is to create an opportunity for everyone to pray. After a few moments (and don't expect that everyone will or needs to pray for each concern), move on to the next concern. Conversational prayer is helpful in using the ACTS format of prayer. You will find this form of prayer non-threatening, allowing individuals who usually are intimidated by praying aloud to become more willing to participate.

Smaller Groups of three or four, particularly if your small group is on the large size, becomes an effective way to give each member an opportunity to participate in prayer. You might have the entire group hear the requests and then break into smaller separate groups of men and women, or have the prayer requests verbalized while in the groups of four or five. Using this format too early in the process of getting to know one another can be threatening to some people, so make sure you know your group. Again, encourage them to use the conversational style of praying so all can participate.

Along with this pattern, early in the life of the group you could have members put a prayer request on a 3x5 card. Each person takes a card and prays for that person throughout the week. Even a phone call for encouragement would be a significant bonding gesture. This lends itself well to group members getting to know each other in a non-threatening, yet energizing way. And, as the group bonds, praying for the person on your right, or left, can be effective.

Prayer Partners can be utilized in various ways. Again, be careful not to use this too soon as some members may shy away from self-disclosure if approached too quickly in the life stage of the group. As trust develops, having prayer partners is a powerful way for individuals to get to know other group members more intimately. This format can happen within the context of the group or outside through various ways. Perhaps a phone call, email or better still, a short visit together over lunch or coffee becomes a significant bonding time. In most groups individuals connect more easily with a few other members and it becomes a natural development. Do not expect that everyone will want to have a prayer partner or a particular prayer partner.

Palms down–Palms up[45] prayer pattern is one way you can utilize different formats that bring creative, fresh worship experiences. There is often the need for quieting minds and relieving stresses and conditions of the day. Palms down, palms up prayer pattern certainly is effective for small group retreats where there is concern about leaving everything that should be done at home. God uses this prayer pattern to prepare His people to listen and respond to Him.

Have your group place their palms down on their knees, ask them to focus on the concerns and distractions of the moment. Turning their palms upward, ask them to surrender these concerns to God, allowing an uncluttered focus on the time together in God's Word. It has a calming effect and the concerns can be revisited during the prayer time if necessary.

Whatever the format or intention, it is wise to keep in mind that thankfully, the Holy Spirit intercedes for us and presents all that needs to be heard to our Awesome, loving Creator God: ". . . the Spirit helps us in our weakness. We do not know what we ought to pray for, but the Spirit himself intercedes for us with groans that words cannot express. And he who searches our hearts knows the mind of the Spirit, because the Spirit intercedes for the saints in accordance with God's will" (Romans 8:26-27).

---

45 Richard Foster, Celebration of Discipline (San Francisco: Harper, 1988), 30-31.

MUSIC

Many small groups are intimidated with the idea of singing with so few voices. Not every group has the privilege of a gifted musician or the availability of an instrument at the meeting place. In the past, having a piano player seemed to be the only option, but today, there are creative and easy ways to experience music in small groups. And, it is important to delegate responsibility to someone in the group exhibiting the gift or the desire for the responsibility. Whatever you choose, balance is important. Not everyone warms up to choruses and many are unfamiliar and uncomfortable with hymns. In choosing the music you use, be creative and use songs that express Who God is and what He has done and, of course, songs that teach correct theology.

Guitar playing is popular. Perhaps there is someone in your group with that ability who is waiting to be asked. Many small groups hand out printed copies of the music for the particular meeting or have a collection of songs or hymnals available each week. Having music and words are obviously helpful, but keep in mind the copyright legalities. If your church has bought a CCLI #, you need to comply with the guidelines of your contract. Making copies of music is illegal without permission.

Including selections from your playlist for the music worship is great fun. Taking the time to select appropriate music with similar themes to the Scripture you have studied allows the response or application to be strongly reinforced. This preparation needs to be delegated to a member who feels drawn or committed to this component of worship. For instance, selecting a song about being in the arms of a loving God solidifies the message of Luke 15 on a welcoming, forgiving Father. Listening to lyrics composed around prayer or Scripture challenges us in our responses. A song about how God changes our name from insecure to confidence can minister deeply. Whether you listen reflectively or join the singing, this implementation of music in this format is worth the effort and provides a natural response to the love of God.

SPIRITUAL AUTOBIOGRAPHY

Spiritual autobiography is another creative and fun way for not only the getting to know you process, but as a means for praising God. We all have a spiritual history whether we are believers in Christ or not. This exercise is exciting to use, for people love to tell stories and people love to hear them! Working on this exercise, for example, over a retreat weekend strengthens the message or topic of the time together, but can also be implemented easily into weekly group meetings. Basically it is telling your story which causes you to examine your life and see some of the ways God has been active. It reminds you how faithful God has been and what He has done in your life over time, and it helps your understanding of where God is urging you to go at the moment. Although easy to do, you might consider using the guidebook "Spiritual Storytelling" from the Spiritual Disciplines series by Dr. Richard Peace[46].

1. Give out large size paper and some colored pens. Have the group recall four or five spiritual highs or spiritual lows throughout their life. Ask them to sketch on the paper something that represents that time. After fifteen minutes of preparation, allow each person five minutes to briefly describe their story. You need to be a gatekeeper of the clock as these stories tend to get longer and longer. I always start and model a short story. I'm no artist so my stick people make people at ease with their sketches. Everyone's story has value and this is a touching exercise for laughter, praise, and even tears.

2. Another form of this exercise takes more time and thought as five minutes to tell a spiritual story isn't really adequate. Small group members should work on their spiritual autobiographies over a period of time. Give some direction. Ask for logical segments of their life. For instance, the divisions might include childhood, young adult, marriage, work, or as an older adult. In each segment have them write about God's impact on their spirituality. Ask them to express how God's presence influenced changes, what they ignored, lessons they learned (yes, the good and the bad) and celebrations they experienced. Encourage them to write creatively with the intention of telling a friend or sharing with their small group. Present the opportunity to do some creative illustrations if they so desire.

Spiritual autobiographies will have to be shared over the course of several weeks. When a group members is given time to share their story, it is important that the remaining group is aware of listening well. Everyone needs to be reminded! Inform the group that while the person is telling their story, each listener should be focusing on the person sharing and not interrupting to ask

---

46 Richard Peace, Adapted from "Pursuit of Wholeness," course at Gordon-Conwell Theological Seminary, Hamilton, Massachusetts, 1995. This course has been included in the spiritual disciplines series published by NavPress and is worth pursuing for the implementation of several spiritual disciplines.

questions or to make comments about incidents. Worse still, listeners should not be thinking about how they can top the story that is being told! Attentive listening doesn't come easily. A few guidelines would be helpful here:

» Silent prayer: ask the Holy Spirit for discernment.
» What did you hear?
» What did you feel while you were listening?
» What might God be showing you through this person?
» When the time is presented, what might you want to say to this person concerning God's leading?
» Is there something you want to speak back to this person: e.g. noticing or feeling or word of encouragement?

Sample spiritual autobiography questions to get people started:

1. Childhood: What did I know about God? In what way did He influence me?
2. Teenage: What was life like for me? How did God play a significant role in my behavior?
3. Ten year segments: What were the opportunities for me to grow spiritually? In what way was God directing me?
4. Marriage: (if applicable) What are some of the struggles? How did/does God help me work through them?
5. Work: (if applicable) What makes it difficult for me to make a stand for Christ? In what way is God helping me at the moment?

Throughout your weeks together, take turns sharing your spiritual autobiographies. Presenting these masterpieces will show the great faithfulness of God in all situations of life. Sharing lives and being listened to is a gift that does not happen very often. The "getting to know you" is a strategic component of group life that is trusted and safe. It becomes a time of knowing and being known, celebrating and being celebrated. God is honored and praised.

CONTEMPLATIVE BIBLE READING

Contemplative Bible reading is one of the oldest methods of Bible study and can be used effectively in times of worship. Its traditional name is lectio divina (lex-ee-oh di-vee-nuh) and is translated as sacred reading, divine reading, or spiritual reading. Contemplative reading and lectio divina are interchangeable terms. Becoming familiar with the process and occasionally using this spiritual discipline tool for worship assists in developing a reflective life.

Many believers spend quality time studying the Bible where significant facts concerning God and theology are accumulated. The tendency is to become human doers. Contemplative Bible reading moves the mind from a more cognitive relationship to the life-transforming goal of holiness. The focus is resting in silence, listening to God, and hearing His Word to us. It is the process of moving the volumes of accumulated knowledge twelve inches from the head to the heart. It is allowing the heart to respond to what the head knows. Contemplative Bible reading paves the way for becoming human beings in communion with our Lord and Maker.

THE PROCESS OF CONTEMPLATIVE BIBLE READING

Contemplative Bible reading is both a simple and a profound way to approach Scripture. It consists of a four-part movement beginning with the text and ending with the prayer. It is a discipline for the individual and for the group as a whole. The following four steps are basic for individual usage and with a few changes in the process, become valuable for group lectio worship. Contemplative Bible reading is a tool for learning to listen to God. When used in a group setting, verbalizing emotions and responses to Scripture aloud among trusting friends creates stronger bonds. Eventually higher trust levels and accountability with one another develops in the group life. The environment is important, so when engaging in this exercise, find a place of quiet, sit straight and attentive, and open your heart and soul to God's voice.

» **Reading/Listening**
Read aloud a short passage of Scripture. As you read, listen for the word or phrase that speaks to you. What is the Spirit drawing your attention to?

» **Meditating**
Repeat aloud the word or phrase to which you are drawn. Make connections between it and your life. What is God saying to you by means of this word or phrase?

» **Praying**

Now take these thoughts and offer them back to God in prayer, giving thanks, asking for guidance, asking for forgiveness, and resting in God's love. What is God leading you to pray?

» **Contemplating**

Move from the activity of prayer to the stillness of contemplation. Simply rest in God's presence. Stay open to God. Listen to God. Remain in peace and silence before God. How is God revealing himself to you?[47]

GROUP CONTEMPLATIVE BIBLE READING

When engaging in this discipline as a group, it becomes a five-step exercise led by a small group leader. The process consists of multiple readings of a short text, individual reflection on that text, brief sharing of this reflection with the small group, and prayer for one another. As the group develops stronger bonds of trust and vulnerability with one another, the process may include breaking into triads for more intimate responses to the Word. The process for groups is as follows: (each step can be introduced by the leader.)

1. Prepare by quieting yourself to listen to God's Word.
2. Listen to the Word of God.
   ▸ As the passage is carefully read twice (leader), listen for the word or phrase that strikes you. During the silence, repeat that phrase softly (or silently) to yourself.
   ▸ When invited, say aloud to the group this word or phrase without comment or elaboration.
3. Ask, "How is my life touched by this word?"
   ▸ The passage is read again (group member). This is followed by personal meditation on how this word or phrase connects to your life.
   ▸ When invited, state in one or two sentences the connection between the phrase and your life.
4. Ask, "Is there an invitation for me to respond to?"
   ▸ After the passage is read a third time (different group member), ponder whether you are being encouraged to do something in response.
   ▸ Share this response briefly with the others.
5. Pray for one another to be able to respond.

---

47 Ibid., Contemplative Bible Reading (Colorado Springs: NavPress, 1998), 12-13. This guidebook is part of the Spiritual Formation series.

Using group contemplative Bible reading is effective not only for praising and thanking God, but is useful for the process of responding to His Word collectively. When we utilize this discipline in personal worship or study, we end by sitting in silence listening to God. In a group setting there is great power in hearing what each of our friends, who share the journey with us, hears. We are challenged not only by our own revelations but also by profound insights and responses of others in the group. An opportunity to hold one another accountable develops. However, the small group leader takes a risk (if the group is not relationally ready) in implementing this discipline in a newly formed, young believer group, so be wise in usage, but when the timing is right, expect the Holy Spirit to begin significant life-change.

CONTEMPLATIVE BIBLE READING EXAMPLE

To illustrate how you use this contemplative Bible reading process, take a look at the Twenty-third Psalm. To spend time with this Scripture in a contemplative posture, it is difficult to read many verses without slowing down, hearing God's voice, pondering, and responding. Consider verse one: "The Lord is my shepherd. I shall not be in want."

Is there a word that causes you to pause, to consider, to be convicted by, or instill a sense of worship? The fact that the Lord is my shepherd is almost over-whelming. What does a good shepherd do? In what way does he care for his sheep? He knows them all by name, he goes after the one missing, stray member of his flock. He guards the door of the pen from all danger. He knows their coming and going. He loving attends their hurts and bruises. He lays down his life for them. The Lord does all this and much more for me. Therefore, I shall not be in want. But I am in want. What is it that I want? Why do I want that? In what way has the Lord provided for me? What lacks in my life that the Lord is unable to provide? Nothing!

THE DISCIPLINE OF SILENCE

Contemplative Bible reading is one spiritual discipline that an individual or group can engage in for interacting with Scripture through listening, meditating, praying, responding, and quietly listening for God's voice. However, silence has become unnatural for us busy, talkative children of God. Often people feel confused and wonder if the voice they hear is really God, themselves, or outside influences. How do we recognize the voice of God? Quieting the heart and refraining from constant chatter takes time and practice. We hear God's voice primarily through Scripture. For this reason, it is essential that we spend time reading and reflecting.

> The simplest guide for knowing when you hear the voice of God is this: Examine what you hear, and if the command or question or comment is patient or kind, it's probably God. If it's boastful or proud or rude or self-seeking, it's probably not God. If it is easily angered or keeping track of wrongs, that could be the Enemy. You can depend on God's Words to embody protection, trust, hope, and perseverance.[48]

> Every time you listen with great attentiveness to the voice that calls you the Beloved, you will discover within yourself a desire to hear that voice longer and more deeply. It is like discovering a well in the dessert. Once you have touched wet ground, you want to dig deeper.[49]

The discipline of silence can also be a form of worship. Leaders usually panic when silence reigns, yet when we worship God and yearn to hear His voice, silence is necessary. The leader can create a comfortable atmosphere for silence and reflection by giving permission for it to happen. Reading Scripture and introducing a short segment of time for silence in order to hear from God is recognizing God's presence; His love and care, the life-transforming power of His Word, and our ability to hear. It also models the importance of silence and rest before God not only with our group of trusted friends, but as we grow in our personal devotional times alone.

Think of silence as the smooth still waters where one can see perfect reflections of the surroundings. With the presence of a slight stirring breeze, the waters become rippled and the reflection is gone. "Silence is the state in which all the powers of the soul and all the faculties of the body are completely at peace, quiet and recollected, perfectly alert yet free from any turmoil or agitation."[50]

> "As long as the soul is not still there can be no vision, but when stillness has brought us into the presence of God, then another sort of silence,

---

48 Jan Johnson, When the Soul Listens (Colorado Springs: NavPress, 1999), 129.

49 Henri Nouwen, Life of the Beloved (New York: Crossroad, 1993), 31.

50 Anthony Bloom, Living Prayer, quoted in Rubin Job and Norman Shawchuck, A Guide to Prayer for Ministers and Other Servants (Nashville: The Upper Room, 1983), 308.

much more absolute, intervenes; the silence of a soul that is not only still and recollected but which is overawed in an act of worship by God's presence; a silence in which, as Julian of Norwich puts it, 'Prayer oneth the soul to God.'"[51]

Whatever the form or exercise, worship is our response to the overtures of love from the heart of our heavenly Father. It is to know and experience the resurrected Christ and the power of the Holy Spirit in a gathered group longing to be transformed. Creative ideas, formats and right techniques may assist in prayer, singing, and verbal expression, but until our spirit unites with the Spirit of God, we have not worshipped the Lord.

Think about your worship experiences. Which ones stand out in your mind and why? Consider your experiences when you initially plan the worship for your small group. Be committed to the time segment designated for worship decided in your covenant and watch for God's blessings.

---

51 Job and Shawchuck, 309.

PRAISING GOD

1. TELL

> » Briefly describe a worship experience that made a lasting impression. What made the experience so memorable?
> » What do you remember about your first prayers to God? Briefly describe. In what way have your prayers developed over time?
> » In what circumstances or environment do you tend to worship God more easily?
> » As a response to this chapter, what new idea of worship would you like to consider for your new small group?

2. DISCUSS

People experience worship in diverse ways, all of which can be powerful in expressing love for God. Discuss among your group concepts from this chapter that might be helpful in creating worship in your new small group. Make suggestions for worship options that were not mentioned.

LIVING SACRIFICES

Read Romans 12:1-2

3. SCRIPTURE:

In the first eleven chapters of the letter to the Romans, Paul has laid out the fundamental doctrines of the Christian faith. He reminds his readers of God's grace and mercy. The "therefore" of Romans 12:1 is there for a reason. We are to respond in faith through what we learn prior to Romans Chapter 12.

Look (observation)

> » Identify some key words in this passage. What does the Scripture say?
> » In what way are we to respond to God's mercy? What might be some actions that God finds "holy and pleasing?"

Think (interpretation)

» What had been the acceptable practice of sacrifices? Briefly describe what the Scripture means by "living" sacrifices. Give an example.
» Paul tells us not to conform to the world. Why is it easy to conform? What are some of the pressures today for conformity?
» How does God renew our minds? Briefly share a personal experience.

Act (application)

» If our minds are renewed, in what way does renewal test and approve what God's will is for us? Give examples.
» Think of one area of your life that could use a bit of renewal. What one step will you take this week to be more pleasing in your being a "living sacrifice?" (if you feel comfortable sharing with your group, do so)

4. PRAYER

For your prayer time, try using either the formats of ACTS or conversational prayer. Challenge each other to personally worship God this week by presenting your bodies as living sacrifices.

5. PREPARATION

Our next chapter will help you with the preparation of your study material. Whether you use a guidebook or construct your own questions, understanding the right questions to ask of Scripture is extremely important for the integrity of your learning and sharing.

Select a discussion leader for your next time together. Read the next chapter and prepare the Bible study before meeting again.

"Love the Lord your God with all your heart,
and with all your soul, and with all your mind,
and with all your strength."

Mark 12

PREPARATION:
UNLOCKING THE SCRIPTURES

"The great doctrines of creation, revelation, redemption, and judgment all imply that man has an inescapable duty both to think and to act upon what he thinks and what he knows."

John Stott, *Your Mind Matters*

How does God's Word speak to us today? In what way does reading Scripture inform us about our faith and grow us spiritually? Do we get absorbed in Scripture as we often do in a good novel and hang on every word? Do we feel consumed with the excitement and developing plot as history unfolds throughout the written Word? What would it feel like if we were able to consume the Bible: to eat it, to chew it, swallow it, digest it, and make it part of us? That is exactly what the prophet Jeremiah imagined about the Word of God when he exclaimed, "When your words came, I ate them; they were my joy and my heart's delight, for I bear your name, O Lord God Almighty" (Jeremiah 15:16).

The little black Bible sat for years on my bedside table. It was a present from my godmother. As a young child, many nights I would open it and randomly read a few words. Feeling I could not understand, it would be closed and for-gotten. It was, however, always in sight, and from time to time, compelled me to peruse the pages. As I reflect on my early years, it is evident that I had been yearning to know if there was a God and if He cared for me.

My spiritual journey started years before I came to know the truth. I thought I was a Christian because I was not Jewish. My family had always attended church, but all I knew about Jesus was in the context of his being a good man. Once I got my driving license, I started visiting various churches to hear what they taught. I was a science major in college and due to the nature of my course work, I was convinced there had to be a creator and that the intricacies of this creation had to be for a purpose. I'm embarrassed to remember asking the chaplain to recommend a book that would tell me what the Bible had to say. And finally, as a young professional working in Boston, a new friend took me to Park Street Church where I heard Dr. Harold J. Ockenga preach the gospel.

For the next eight months, I heard answers to the many questions of life that I had so yearned to know. It all came together for me at a Billy Graham Crusade where Dr. Graham described my desperate condition. He explained that when the Holy Spirit dwells in you through belief in Jesus Christ, God's Word would become more clear and powerful. Life-transformation happens! And, that was my experience. While alone in my apartment that night, I cried out to God with confession and trust, asking to become His child forever. Scripture began to make sense and my spiritual journey was exciting as I delved into the Word, allowing it to shape and reshape me continually for years to come. I became confident that the Holy Spirit lives and breathes in the pages of God's Word and that those who seek with humility and compassion to understand the simple, yet often challenging texts, will find truth and see God.

One of my favorite passages of Scripture is the account of two disciples of Jesus walking the Emmaus road. When Jesus joins them, they do not recog-nize him. Jesus explains the Scriptures and what they say about himself. Finally their eyes are opened and they recognized Jesus just as he disappeared from their sight. With apparent awe and enthusiasm, they exclaimed, "Were not our hearts burning within us while he talked with us on the road and opened the Scriptures to us?" (Luke 24:32). This episode in Luke's gospel gives flesh to Jeremiah's metaphor of reading and eating. "The holy book that must be learned, marked, read, and inwardly digested is in the end no book at all. It is the very person of the Incarnate One, the Word made flesh, at once the interpreter of the book and its subject."[52]

HISTORICAL PERSPECTIVE

In the sixteenth century, the Reformers declared their confidence in the perspicuity of Scripture. This sometimes difficult word to pronounce simply means "clarity." What they were saying was that Scripture is basically clear and simple enough for any literate person, and one who has the Holy Spirit within, to understand the basic message (1 Corinthians 2:11, 1 John 2:27). In fact, some areas of Scripture are so clear and simple that they become offensive to those who pride themselves with intellectualism. It is not to say that many areas of Scripture are not difficult and controversial, but according to the Reformer Martin Luther, the difficult and obscure passages were usually stated more clearly and simply in other parts of Scripture. In other words, the Reformers stressed that "Scripture interprets Scripture."

During the Reformation, initially there was a major concern about small groups meeting together and studying Scripture without theologians in attendance. And today, the great fear of shared ignorance threatens the value of lay-led Bible study. This is a legitimate concern. R.C. Sproul, theologian and writer, states: "One of the most significant developments of the lay renewal movement has been the advent of small home Bible study groups. Laymen teach each other or pool their own ideas in these Bible studies. Such groups have been quite successful in renewing the church. They will be even more so as the people are beginning to open up the Bible and study it together. But it is also an exceedingly dangerous thing. Pooling of knowledge is edifying to the church; pooling of ignorance is destructive and can manifest the problem of the blind leading the blind."[53]

The Reformers were committed to forming small groups of laypeople to study Scripture to help implement theology in faith and practice. The leaders, however, were comprised of Teaching Elders. They were well trained in theology and proper study skills, and understood the value of approaching Scriptures with integrity. That is not usually the case today with our small groups so it is

---

52 Roger Ferlo, Opening the Bible (Cambridge, Massachusetts: Cowley Publications, 1997), 13.

53 R.C. Sproul, Knowing Scripture (Downers Grove: InterVarsity, 1977), 41. This important work should be included in your "study tools" as the method of interpretation is thoroughly explored.

critical that as leaders, we understand the rudiments of biblical study for proper understanding and application.

Although small group leaders are not considered small group teachers, we are ultimately responsible as designated leaders, or facilitators, for approaching the Bible study time together. Perhaps you have the gift of teaching. That is a precious gift, but keep in mind that the purpose of your small group is to enable everyone to participate in discovering God's Word through study and group discussion. As a leader, understanding how to study the Bible is important whether you use a guidebook or construct your own questions. Setting aside a time for your group to participate in the skills of Bible study you have learned will also be a significant contribution for helping others study with integrity.

God reveals Himself and His time-spanning truth to us in the Bible. If we really want to know God and know His will for our lives, we should hunger and thirst for His Word. Discovering God's truth is an exciting process. The Holy Spirit opens the eyes of our hearts to see what God wants us to learn. We look closely at the words, we think through the meaning and significance and we act on the commands and truths to grow spiritually with God and with others. The inductive Bible study method is one helpful process for leaders to understand for reading and reflecting on God's Word. It involves learning the right questions to ask of the Scripture. The basics of observation, interpretation, and application are transferable with every book of the Bible or type of study you decide to explore.

SCRIPTURE TO CONSIDER:

Open my eyes, that I may see wonderful things in your law (Psalm 119:18).

All Scripture is God-breathed and is useful for teaching, rebuking, correcting, and training in righteousness, so that the man of God may be thoroughly equipped for every good work (II Timothy 3:16-17).

Therefore, I urge you, brothers, in view of God's mercy to offer your bodies as living sacrifices, holy and pleasing to God–this is your spiritual act of worship. Do not conform any longer to the pattern of this world, but be transformed by the renewing of your mind. Then you will be able to test and approve what God's will is–his good, pleasing and perfect will (Romans 12:1-2).

BIBLE STUDY TOOL BOX

Every serious student of the bible needs to have tools to help the study process. Most of us are not professional Bible scholars and these tools will help to keep us on track as we dive into God's Word on our own or with a group. Here is a list that might be helpful to you:

1. Have two or three different translations to compare texts.
2. Include a paraphrase to help with the central message. Paraphrases are not translations.
3. It is better to use paraphrases after initial study of Scripture.
4. Choose two or three reliable commentaries for assisting in interpretation.
5. Bible dictionary
6. Bible atlas
7. Handbook of life in biblical times.

As you begin your study, ask the Holy Spirit to open your eyes and ears to God's Word as He is the one who guides us into all truth. Identify the author and the purpose of the book by reading the entire book in one sitting. You might need the help of a Bible commentary or study Bible to assist you in the historical background, important culture, or political arena. Remember not to consult the commentary for individual verses until you have done your homework.

The Bible is not just one book. It is 66 books. And there isn't one set way to study all the different genres. So it is important for you to identify the type of book you are studying so your study approach is appropriate. For example, is it poetry (psalms), historical (Kings, Acts), narrative (Luke), letter (Ephesians), prophecy (Daniel, Revelation), Wisdom (proverbs)? Understanding these genres of the Bible will determine how you approach the Scriptures. If you choose to do a character study, topical study, or biblical theme, it is important that you understand the proper context for each verse or groupings of verses.

As you begin your Bible study, make sure you come confidently believing Scripture is truth. Unfortunately, much of the surrounding culture is committed to the world-view that represents no absolutes and chooses to accept truth as relative. However, the Bible and its truth is the foundation on which to place both faith and action. To know God's Word takes a bit of persistence and dedication on your part.

One problem facing small group leadership seems to be that many have never been shown how to study Scripture properly. It is common to hear, "I just don't know how to start to study the Bible. It's hit or miss with me I'm afraid!" It is often said that if you aim at nothing, you'll hit it every time... and with the lack of direction, with unhealthy methods of study and interaction with God's Word, we are apt to miss the proper interpretation of God's Word.

IMPEDIMENTS TO EFFECTIVE BIBLE STUDY

There are inadequate approaches to the study of God's Word that do not nurture us. Although God's Word is powerful and penetrating, if you do not know how to approach Scripture with integrity and if you do not understand the dangers of Scripture twisting and misuse, you will not only deprive yourselves of the power of God's Word, but will be agents of spreading shared ignorance. Take a look at the following methods commonly used for personal Bible study.

» **The Consultation Approach**
"I have a problem... the Bible must have an answer... where is there a verse for my particular problem?" There are many promises and verses of encouragement in the Bible, but using this method for daily devotional study is too selective. Take time to read the surrounding verses to know the proper context in order to determine if the Scripture does apply to you.

» **The Vitamin Pill Approach**
"A few verses a day drives Satan away!" It is good advice to meditate on a Scripture verse or two during the day, but this process hardly taps into the depth of the surrounding Scripture or allows for the proper context for understanding. However, using a devotional with subject headings that include the lexicon can be quite edifying.[54]

» **The Consecutive Approach**
"If a few verses are good ... full chapters must be better." This is a good beginning for the study of a particular book. An overview is important to pick up the big idea of the contents. When reading an entire chapter, make sure you know the surrounding context, but

---

54 Devotional suggestion: Ruben P. Job and Norman Shawchuck, A Guide To Prayer For Ministers & Other Servants (Nashville: The Upper Room). This guide includes weekly themes, daily Scripture readings, and selected quotes from various authors.

remember ... more is not always better. For example, reading three chapters of a book each day to stay on a yearly track often causes us to focus on getting the job done rather than the power of the Scripture and its message.

» **The Devotional Approach**

"I read from a devotional book every day!" Reading what authors have to say about a verse limits your biblical insights to the author's biblical insights. Devotional readings, however, can be instructive and encouraging. It is a method that is useful, but should not be the only Scriptural input you experience. Do not base your understanding on what God has told other people; allow God to speak to you.

» **The Magical Approach**[55]

"Open the Bible and point. That's the message God has for me today?" There certainly are times when we receive encouragement from God by using this method. It can, however, be a dangerous process of inaccurate application. Since this is a prevalent habit of many, it is worth taking a good look at the implications of this approach.

While in her twenties, my good friend had been diagnosed with Non-Hodgkin's Lymphoma. The prognosis was poor and there was little hope of survival. Opening her Bible one morning, she allowed her finger to drop on the open page and there claimed the verse for her struggle against cancer: "You will not die," the Scripture stated.

Many believers use this practice to find the Scripture for their day. Is it wrong? Is there truth in this method? Is the Scripture misleading? A good student of the Bible will quickly recognize that applying Scripture out of its proper context is misleading and often dangerous. Perhaps the Scripture does pertain to the current situation in which you find yourself, but using this method of hearing from God is lacking in proper biblical approach and understanding. In my friend's case, there was a fifty-fifty chance of it being right. In fact, now, many years later, she remains healthy and praises God for sparing her life.

Using this method of approaching Scripture does not help develop good study habits that allow for accurate interpretation and application. Take a

---

55 Richard Peace, "Inductive Bible Study," a course attended at Gordon-Conwell Theological Seminary, 1995. The six descriptions have been modified.

moment to experience the Magical method and discover what Scripture is telling you at the moment. Open your Bible and pretend your finger landed on Matthew 27:5. Read the message for you today. You don't like that message? Perhaps if you read Luke 10:37 it will help clarify what Scripture is encouraging you to do. Didn't like that one either? Let's try one more time. Read John 13:27. I'm sure you are thinking at this point that none of these verses were meant for you today! This simple exercise reinforces the necessity for proper study skills as we focus our minds on God's Word, allowing his Word to instruct, convict, encourage, and empower.

Sadly there is an impression among many believers that a person cannot discern truth objectively and therefore rely on others to interpret for them. Often this results in only one voice being heard. When differing interpretations present themselves, questions are raised: "Which voice is correct?" Understanding how to study the Bible is critical if we are to know God through His Word. He promises to write His Word in our minds and on our heart so that we might be imitators of Him. It is a process. Scripture teaches us doctrine, allows us to see areas in our thoughts and actions that need correction, and leads us in developing an authentic Christian mindset as God prepares us for His ministry. Now, let's investigate the process of inductive study which allows us to approach the Scriptures with integrity.

ASKING THE RIGHT QUESTIONS OF THE SCRIPTURE

King David cried out to God, "O God, you are my God, earnestly I seek you; my soul thirsts for you, my body longs for you, in a dry and weary land where there is no water" (Psalm 63:1). In what way do you thirst and long for God? The Reformers fought long and hard to bring the Scriptures to the common people in order to make disciples for Jesus Christ. Today it feels like we are living in a dry and weary land where there is no water. Yet, we have been given the powerful privilege of becoming a "priesthood of believers" (1 Peter 2:9). The Bible is within our grasp to read, study, meditate upon, and respond to as we long to see renewal within our churches and communities. Asking the right questions of Scripture through the Inductive Bible study process is one tool we can learn and utilize as we commit to studying the Scriptures with integrity.

The word inductive describes reasoning which proceeds from basic facts to conclusions. It is a common thought process we use every day as we make decisions. The flip side of inductive study is deductive. The difference? Dr. Merrill C.

Tenney clearly contrasts the two types of study this way: "induction is the logic of discovery while deduction is the logic of proof."[56] For our purposes, we will use the inductive method to discover every detail we can in order to construct the accurate interpretation for applying the Scripture appropriately.

Reading the entire book of the Bible you have chosen to study is always recommended with the inductive process. It is during this reading that you will start gathering details you will need for your future analysis. By putting together various complements that lead to the big picture, you should be asking the observation question, "What does the Scripture say?" moving into the interpretation question, "What does the Scripture mean?" and finally "How will I respond to what I have learned?" The process involves the three steps of observation, interpretation, and application.

Often a significant omission in small group Bible study material is the focus on application. So whether you use a guidebook or construct the study yourself, the inductive method is essential for the proper understanding of and the response to the Scripture your small group is studying. It will also help you evaluate a potential guidebook you are considering for your group.

TAKING A GOOD LOOK

Observation: "What does the Scripture say?"

First, identify the type of literature you are reading as it will eventually make a difference in your interpretation process. For instance, is the passage a letter, speech, poem, parable, narrative? Read the entire book in one sitting if possible. As you begin to observe the big idea and main topics, take notes of what you learn. Later, when you reread passage by passage, there are important questions to ask of the text. "What does the Scripture say" is an important first step for understanding. Use these familiar "W" words as prompts.

1. **Who** is the author of the book? What can you learn about the author? To whom is the author writing? Who are the major and minor characters? What part do they play?
2. **Where** do the events take place? If there are references to towns, cities, provinces, or place of activity, take note. If you are unfamiliar with

---

56 Dr. Merrill C. Tenney, quoted in Hans Finzel, Opening The Book (Wheaton, Illinois: Victor Books, 1987), 15.

the names, look them up in a Bible atlas or map in the back of your Bible. If you are reading a letter, where do the recipients live? What is significant about this area or church?

3. **When** does this interaction take place? Are there dates, times, references to events that are mentioned?

4. **What** actions or events are taking place? What words or ideas are being repeated? What is the big idea or theme that is central to the discourse? What is the mood? What does the author want the readers to hear?

5. **Why** is the passage included? Is there a problem being addressed? Are there explanations, statements or reasons for the Scripture?

6. **How** is the passage written? Are there literary devices such as figures of speech that are important for proper understanding? How are the readers hearing this message?

Once we have asked these questions about the Scripture we are considering, we are well equipped with a strong foundation for the next step of interpretation. Be very careful not to move too fast to the next step, however, as you want to be well informed with the facts. Spend lots of time with the observation process for the more we observe, the better our interpretation and application will be. If you have recorded your findings, you can refer to them as you continue through the rest of the study process. The why question will become an important step for accurate interpretation later in the process.

At first this exercise seems very tedious and time consuming (and it is), but eventually your mind will be trained to go through the process. Each time you read a particular Scripture, you will find something else you have missed; new and exciting discoveries. So "train your eyes to see the obvious and the not so obvious."[57]

For our purposes in unlocking the Scriptures, understanding the Bible literally is important. The Bible is a book. It needs to be read and understood as a book. Literal basically signifies the structure of letters or words. Therefore, we need to look at the words for face value. "To interpret the Bible literally

---

57 James F. Nyquist and Jack Kuhatschek Leading Bible Discussions (Downers Grove: InterVarsity Press, 1985), 26. This is a concise book with essentials for leading group discussions. Inductive process for study is clear and informative.

is to interpret it as literature. That is, the natural meaning of a passage is to be interpreted according to the normal rules of grammar, speech, syntax and context".[58]

In response to the above comment, when a literary device, such as figure of speech is used, we move from the literal face value of the words to what the author meant by choosing the words he did. That's the challenge. For instance, if I read, "the whole Judean countryside and all the people of Jerusalem went out to see him" (Mark 1:5), I need to recognize the use of figurative language, the hyperbole, Mark uses to make a profound statement. Most likely it was not the whole Judean countryside or all the people of Jerusalem who went to see John the Baptist, but it paints a powerful picture of the immense interest in seeing and hearing this man sent by God.

So during the observation process, take note of the various figures of speech before you start the interpretation process. With thoughtful consideration, many significant truths will be discovered that are missed when one glances quickly over the literary style. Your challenge will be to unravel the purpose the author had in using that particular figure of speech. The following are a few of the common figures of speech you will encounter.

FIGURES OF SPEECH[59]

1. **Comparison** is stating something that is the same (James 3:4-5). James is talking about how powerful the tongue can be. He compares the large ships driven by strong winds that are steered by small rudders to the human body that is often badly controlled by a small tongue.

2. **Contrast** is stating something that is different (1 John 1:5). John uses contrasts many times. "God is light. In Him there is no darkness." He continues to make the contrast of light and dark, lies and truth, sinfulness and purification.

3. **Simile** is a direct comparison and often preceded by the word like or as (Psalm 1:3).

---

58 Sproul, Knowing Scripture, 48-49.
59 Adapted from Richard Peace, "Inductive Bible Study" course.

The psalmist is commending the man who loves God's Word and meditates on it day and night rather than listening to unrighteous men considered wicked: "He is like a tree planted by streams of water." We all know that trees are healthy and strong when they have a nutritional source of water.

4. **Metaphor** is an implied comparison of likeness and usually easy to discern (John 6:48).
   "I am the bread of life" is an example of the many "I am" statements of Jesus. We can easily understand what he was trying to convey to his listeners and to us today.
   There are, however, cases where Jesus used a metaphor that, unfortunately, has continued to cause great divisions within the Christian church. Using (Luke 22:19), Jesus states, "This is my body" what did he mean? Did he mean this statement in a literal sense or in a metaphorical sense? The Reformers, John Calvin and Martin Luther, were never able to resolve this issue and there remains today different theological interpretations concerning the Eucharist celebration. So metaphors bring a set of additional challenges, but for the most part, one is able to discern the implied comparison.

5. **Hyperbole** is an exaggeration. It is used to make an impression just as an exclamation point would. It draws your attention to the seriousness of the comment (Matthew 5:29).
   When Jesus said "If your right eye causes you to sin, gouge it out and throw it away," is he actually suggesting that you harm yourself or is the inference focused on the importance of self scrutiny for living a set apart, blameless life?

6. **Personification** gives life to abstract, inanimate objects (Isaiah 55:12). When God's Word accomplishes His purpose, we will go forth in joy and peace and "the mountains and hills will burst into song… and all the trees of the field will clap their hands."

SPOTTING KEY WORDS

Understanding the words you read is critical, for it is here where much of the interpretation is derived. It is important to use a modern translation of good reputation and is best to refrain from using a paraphrase for word studies.

When there is a word you do not know, look it up in a lexicon or dictionary and write down the definition. Do not come to early conclusions on your interpretation before you complete the tedious work of observation.

Determining the context of a particular word is strategic in understanding the meaning of the word. I appreciate this example my friends included in a workshop. "How would you define the word 'run?' I'm going for a run, would you run to the store for me, I scored a home run, I have a run in my stocking, the Patriots are on a run, my nose is running'?"[60] This example shows us the various possibilities of word meanings and therefore demands that we know the proper context in which to interpret the correct meaning of the particular word.

A biblical example is found in Matthew 6: 25-27. Directly following Jesus' words "Therefore I tell you, do not worry about your life" he states, "Is not life more important than food?" and following that, "Who of you by worrying can add a single hour to his life?" The word "life" is used three times and has three different meanings. Doing a word study[61] would help you understand that in this particular text Jesus talks about life as the existence one is experiencing, the essence of life in a sense of the soul, or eternal life, and finally the span of life one might have. Two of the three words translated as "life" differ with Greek roots and understanding. Without this close observation, the Scripture even seems to be contradictory.

REPETITION

Repeated words signify what the author wants to stress. When you see the same word, or several similar words throughout a section of Scripture, it is a clue that the author really wants you to understand the message they convey. Always keep track of words that are repeated as it provides good information for your interpretation process. For example, in Psalm 121:1-8, the psalmist repeats the word "watch" five times in eight short verses. Being aware of the repetition drives home the message that God provides for you without ceasing.

---

60 Catherine Beckerleg and Elizabeth Shively, "Unlocking the Scriptures Workshop," 2002.

61 Using Hebrew/Greek Bible with word definitions included explains the proper Hebrew or Greek word and its meaning and often better defines words that the English language struggles to verbalize.

UNUSUAL WORDS

Train your eyes to take note of the words that are strong and striking. Notice words that stand out from others like sin, demons, death, fire, wrath, as well as love, protection, grace, salvation, eternal life. These words can be considered content-laden and include the Christian jargon of justification, sanctification, eternal life, and all those words we believers use easily that none of our unbelieving friends quite understand. You might consider Romans 8:29 where Paul uses the words foreknew, predestined, firstborn, called, justified, and glorified. What is Paul saying? Define the words and know what they mean. Writing down the proper definition forces you to be articulate.

GRAMMATICAL STRUCTURE

When a verse starts with therefore, it is there for a reason. Words such as therefore, but, and, because of that, for this reason, and since then, set up conditions or refer to something said prior to the particular verse in question. So here we again must remember to put verses into the proper context. Context is king! Know what comes before and after a section of Scripture. For example, the third chapter of Colossians begins, "Since, then…" and continues with the rules for holy living. Since what? If we look back to the second chapter, we find the explanation of our redemption through Christ being nailed on the cross. And "since he has accomplished that for us…", as children of God, there are expectations of our behavior.

MOVEMENT WITH TIME AND PLACE

Carefully watching the passage of time by days, months, leadership reigns, or various changes of geographical locations mentioned is important to the observation process. For example, how old was Daniel was when he was thrown into the lion's den? Most Sunday School curriculum portrays Daniel in this situation as a handsome, young, strapping youth. Daniel, however, was 82 or 83. Most people don't like to hear this information as it requires a bit of rethinking. By watching the time passage of the kings and their reigns; "twelve months later" (Daniel 4:28), and "in the first year of King Belshazzar" (Daniel 7:1) we better understand the passage of time. And, you might discover that Noah and his companions were not on the ark for forty rainy days and nights. It was approximately one year and four months before they stepped upon the drying soil. It is important to observe the words that signify the passage of time.

Understanding the significance of towns, cities, and provinces is also important to aid accurate interpretation. For example, in Mark 5 we read about Jesus crossing the Sea of Galilee to Gerasenes. Learning about this town and finding that it is part of the Decapolis, ten cities, we discover that Jesus is now in a Gentile territory. Furthermore, the word pig is a significant word and is mentioned several times. This conveys the livelihood of the residents. That in itself tells us that it was not a Jewish community. These are important details to gather as you understand more fully the scope of the narrative story.

OBSERVATION IN SUMMARY:

» Identify the type of literature
» Read the book in one sitting if possible
» Discover the historical context, political arena, culture
» Observe themes that surface with an overview of the book
» Understand the figurative languages and purpose
» Define unfamiliar words
» Notice any repetitions
» Understand the grammatical structure in opening statements
» Pay attention to the passage of time and places

Having collected valuable observation information, you are now ready to move on to the next step of interpretation.

DISCERNING THE MEANING

Interpretation: "What does the Scripture mean?"

The goal for interpretation is to figure out what the passage of Scripture means. All the biblical facts you have accumulated will be meaningless until you find the relationship between them. This requires your getting into the brain of the author, to know his attitude, thoughts, motives, and emotions as he records statements. At this point you are not asking what does this mean to me? It is here where the threat of shared ignorance comes into play. When you read Scripture and ask what it means to you without the proper steps of interpretation skills, you might be jumping into hasty conclusions as we all have preconceived ideas and traditions that influence our understanding. You are asking, "What does the Scripture mean?"

You will often see the words exegesis and hermeneutics when interpretation is involved. These are fancy theological terms that confuse people into thinking that they need to be biblical scholars in order to derive accurate interpretations. Basically both terms signify the plain meaning of the text through careful study and enlightened common sense. Just as we ask the observation questions daily, (especially if you have teenagers), "Where are you going?" "With whom are you driving?" "How will you get there?" "What will you be doing?", we strive to find the meaning in every day experiences. Common sense gives us direction. Having said that, interpretation is not always easy and takes considerable thought.

"Meaning, significance and explanation are the goals of interpretation. How do you reach these goals? Once you have made your conclusions, how do you know that you are not mistaken? We all have heard comments like, 'that's your idea of what the passage says, but to me it is very different. You have your interpretation and I have mine, and mine is as good as yours!' The person is half right, for many people will not agree on the same interpretation, but just because there are many different interpretations of a passage, it does not mean they are all good interpretations. A good interpretation must pass one crucial test; it must conform to the author's intended meaning. But if it is different from the author's intended meaning, it is incorrect."[62]

The above statement says it all. You have work to do. The question of interpretation is not left up to you to infer a meaning that relates well to you, but to discover the purpose or motivation of the author to say what he says. Finding out the proper interpretation involves making sure you know the significance of your observation list by asking a few more questions. "Did I have any problems with the text?" "Do I understand the words that were used?" "Did I understand the figurative language as I attempt to interpret?"

Interpretation is not easy and needs to be accurate. Though it is true that God, through the power of His Holy Spirit, allows one to interpret and apply as he or she reads through Scripture, many a great theologian has spent hours on their knees in confusion storming the heavens with prayer for God to open their eyes to the truth of His Word.

Understanding the grammatical style and checking out the importance of

---

62 Adapted from Leading Bible Discussions, 27.

the appropriate history and culture prepares you to make some attempts at the proper interpretation. Thinking back to the emphasis of the Reformers, "Scripture interprets Scripture," if you come up with an interpretation that no one else has ever discovered, it would be best to discard it. And, never base your interpretation on an obscure passage of Scripture. Knowing that Scripture supports other Scripture, you will always find passages that reinforce your interpretation when the process is completed correctly.

"The aim of good interpretation is simple: to get at the 'plain meaning of the text.' And the most important ingredient one brings to that task is enlightened common sense. The test of good interpretation is that it makes good sense of the text. Correct interpretation, therefore, brings relief to the mind as well as a prick or prod to the heart."[63] Bringing culture, traditional background, personal experiences along with prior understanding of words or ideas can impose the dangers of inaccurate interpretation. Perhaps without realizing it, students of the Bible are led astray or have imported various foreign ideas into the text. You cannot make Scripture say what you want it to say and it cannot contradict comparable Scripture. A text cannot mean what it never meant. By utilizing careful observation skills, the original meaning of most texts will be discovered.

As you begin the interpretation process, ask once again the who, what, where, when, why, and how questions addressed in the observation process. "The difference between observation and interpretation is that in observation you must stay within the boundaries of a pericope (particular section of Scripture being studied), while in interpretation the surrounding context, indeed, the whole Bible and more, is fair game. In observation, you act as a bystander coming upon a scene, attempting to piece together the facts. In interpretation, you become a probing detective attempting to dig even deeper to make sense of your findings."[64]

EXAMPLE OF MISINTERPRETED SCRIPTURE

For an example of common misuse of Scripture, take a look at Matthew 18:20: "For where two or three come together in my name, there am I with them." This Scripture often endorses the motivation for church annual meetings, committee meetings, prayer meetings, and even small groups. Applying

---

63 Fee and Stuart, 16.

64 Jeffrey Arnold, Discovering The Bible For Yourself (Downers Grove: InterVarsity Press, 1993), 63-64.

this Scripture for these reasons is taken out of context and is not the reason Jesus said those words.

Have you ever questioned why the "two or three" is explicitly stated? Why not just "one?" In what way did it interest you to find out why Jesus said what he said? Scripture consistently tells us that we are not alone; the Holy Spirit is with us as believing individuals and as groups. So why did Jesus say "two or three?" Let's find out.

Upon careful observation the "two or three" should have caught our attention. It is an important statement and must be explored. In doing so, one realizes that Matthew 18:15-20 concerns church discipline. If we use a cross reference, (allowed in interpretation), we will find the book of Deuteronomy very important. Here Scripture is relating the Law of Moses in the process of convicting a person for criminal or offensive behavior. "One witness is not enough to convict a man accused of any crime or offense he may have committed. A matter must be established by the testimony of two or three witnesses" (Deuteronomy 19:15).

Remembering that Jesus' life and teaching were during the Old Testament covenantal time frame, Jesus is applying the process stated in Deuteronomy to criminal and offensive acts for the emerging Christian church. Church discipline requires that two or three witnesses be established for the carefully prepared process of church discipline. And as God implied within this context that He would be present guiding the decisions with His wisdom, so Jesus implies that his presence gives authority and answers to that which the two or three persons have prayed.

Once again we find the conviction process mentioned in Hebrews 10:28; "Anyone who rejected the law of Moses died without mercy on the testimony of two or three witnesses." The context for this verse is to persevere in the Christian faith by acting in the hope of the gospel rather than leading a life continued in sin. Here is a figure of speech. The author compares the punishment of the sinners in Deuteronomy to the rejection of the gospel. These three passages, Deuteronomy 19:15, Matthew 18:20, and Hebrews 10:28 are related and each reinforces the interpretation of the other. So, when you justify gathering for a prayer meeting using the Scripture reference of Matthew 18:20 confirming that Jesus is present during the time together, it is correct in theology, but incorrect for this particular Scripture interpretation and application.

The importance of approaching the Scripture with integrity not only trains us in proper study skills but helps to prevent the dreaded shared ignorance. Getting in the mind of the writer so you know why he wrote what he wrote and to whom it was written is critical for finding the correct application.

INTERPRETATION IN SUMMARY:

» After gathering all the facts, make sure you understand the significance of words, phrases, and literary uses.
» Look for the "big idea" and supporting complements.
» Discern the reason for the author's purpose in writing the book.
» Consider how the readers would "hear" what was written.
» Come to a conclusion as to what the Scripture implied to the hearers.

And, don't forget to ask these questions:

» Is my interpretation consistent with theme, purpose and structure of the book?
» Is my interpretation consistent with other Scriptures about the same subject or is there a glaring difference?
» Am I considering the historical and cultural context?

After, and only after you have done your homework, it might be helpful to consult a good commentary or other available study tools for better understanding the Scripture. Now you are ready to make the connection to life and practice.

MAKING THE NECESSARY CONNECTIONS

Application: "How will I respond?"

Often small groups do well with the gathering of information and finding the implied interpretation. Where weakness surfaces is with the actual doing part of the study. The purpose of studying Scripture is not to collect volumes of information and great ideas, but to allow the Holy Spirit to transform lives through experiencing the knowledge accumulated. We are challenged throughout Scripture to have the "mind of Christ" (1 Peter 4:1). Here we move the information twelve inches or so from our head to our heart. If we have done our investigation properly, we will understand the issues of the biblical culture and problems of that time.

Certain books of the Bible do not have a direct application to us today. Much of this Scripture is found in the Old Testament. There will, however, most likely be a general principle that will. If the specific principle does not apply to us, finding the general principle will then challenge us to the so what? of the study. We need to ask ourselves and our small group, "What we will do differently because we have studied this particular Scripture?" There are guidelines to follow for this application question:

Rule #1   Whenever our situation corresponds to that faced by the original readers, God's Word to us is exactly the same as it was to them.

Rule #2   Whenever our situation does not correspond to that faced by the original readers, we should look for the principle underlying God's Word to them. We can then apply that principle to comparable situations today.[65]

"Learning to generalize is one of the most important steps in applying the Bible. When, on the surface, a passage seems to have little application to our situation today, we need to look beneath the surface for a general principle."[66] The importance of understanding the culture at the time of the writing wraps the Scripture in reality. Most always there is a general principle for us to consider as we strive to know the heartbeat of Jesus. So again, a handbook explaining life during biblical times can be useful.

It is evident that asking particular important questions of the Scripture allows better interpretation and application. Understanding Scripture and responding to what is read, however, should not be governed by strict skills, regulations, and procedures. God's Word is living, active, and powerfully changes lives without organized process. However, once you understand the right questions to ask and develop the disciplines, whether you are aware or not, your mind keeps looking for the not so obvious and Scripture comes alive in new and different ways. Scripture that you thought you knew well surfaces additional and sometimes different life-changing challenges.

---

65 Nyquist and Kuhatschek,, 34.

66 Ibid, 52.

Application in summary: the response to Scripture

» What did the passage mean in its original context?
» What does the passage say to our society today?
» What does the passage say to us as individuals?
» In what way will I obey this command?
» How does this promise work into my life?
» What is this telling me about the sin in my life?
» How can I give thanks and praise?
» What does this tell me about God, Jesus, the Holy Spirit, others, and myself?

Once again, an excellent ending question to your time together would be this challenge: "Considering what we have learned, is there something specific can we do or do differently because we studied this Scripture?" It is important to remember the attributes of knowing, loving, serving, admonishing, and celebrating for creating authentic Christian community. Accountability is important. Challenging one another with one step we will take this week provides the environment for checking in with one another the following week.

If we are to be leaders of integrity and if we strive to use good tools for understanding and applying the Scripture, then we are on our way to spiritual renewal. Our small groups will be stimulating and challenging, our spiritual journeys exciting and God will be honored.

UNLOCKING THE SCRIPTURES

I. TELL

Every day brings new temptations. Briefly describe a time when you were tempted by something exciting, but knew in your heart that it was wrong. What influenced your final decision?

2. DISCUSS

Discuss the value of the new Bible study tools you discovered in this chapter. Was there an "aha" moment? Identify it. Did you experiment with the various skills suggested? If so, what did you learn? In the past, in what way have you been discouraged while searching the Scriptures? Did you identify with any method listed as an impediment? If so, which one?

OVERCOMING TEMPTATIONS

Read Matthew 4:1-11

3. SCRIPTURE

John the Baptist has been preparing the way for Jesus' ministry. Fulfilling Scripture, John has just baptized Jesus. A voice from heaven exclaimed, "This is my Son, whom I love; with him I am well pleased." At this point, Jesus is led into the desert and becomes a model for us concerning our daily life temptations.

Look (observation)

- » Who are the characters in this portion of Scripture?
- » Where does this take place and what is important about this location?
- » What are the temptations and how does Jesus respond?
- » Are there any repeated words, phrases, or figures of speech? If so, briefly describe.

Think (interpretation)

- » What is the purpose and meaning of this Scripture?
- » Considering your answers to the above observations, how will the

original readers hear this passage?

» What does Matthew want all readers to understand?

Act (application)

» Are there specific principles or general principles included? If so, in what way are they transferable to our culture today? The significance?
» What new information or encouragement did you discover in this passage?
» In what way will you consider temptations differently because of this study?
» Name one step you will take to implement this Scripture into your life.

4. PRAYER

Take time to pray for one another. Is there a temptation you are facing at the moment? In what way might your small group friends support you this week in prayer? As you disclose temptation issues, be accountable to each other next week with the progress you have made. You have been together for six weeks and the trust level should be growing if you have continued with the sharing and self-disclosure segments of the training course. The important attributes of knowing, loving, serving, admonishing, and celebrating are essential for healthy small group life. Celebrate as you grow spiritually through the accountability process together.

5. PREPARATION

Always end the discussion time with the challenge of response. Keep in mind, if you do not keep your group moving along through your lesson, you are certain to run out of time and take the risk that these questions will not be considered. Spending time on constructing effective questions or evaluating and reworking questions in a guidebook, if necessary, is also an important step in creating good dialogue. Thought provoking questions make a significant difference in the enthusiasm and response during small group discussion.

Our next chapter will help you see more clearly the importance of constructing and utilizing proper questions throughout the various stages of growth the group is bound to experience. Preparing or recognizing questions that help a group achieve their goals and purposes create healthy group process. And life-transformation and renewal happens in healthy small groups.

Select the discussion leader for your next group meeting and read carefully the following chapter. Prepare the Bible study.

"Do not conform any longer to the pattern of this world, but be transformed by the renewing of your mind. Then you will be able to test and approve what God's will is—his good, pleasing and perfect will."

Romans 12:2

INTERACTION: CREATING EFFECTIVE DISCUSSION

"Jesus was a brilliant teacher. He knew how to tell a story that would propel people into thinking in new categories. He was king of the one-liner. And He understood the power of a well-timed, well-phrased question."

Karen Lee-Thorp, *How To Ask Great Questions*

Feeling uncertain but excited, I sat around the table with sixteen young people eager to be in a small group. I had responded to a request from some of the young 20 somethings who had asked for cross-generational leaders to lead a few of their small groups. I knew that these young people wanted spiritual mentoring, but I also knew the older, more spiritually mature leaders would benefit from the energy of the younger believers as well. Still, I wondered why I had put myself in this situation with a new group, all of whom were younger than my children, and none of whom I knew. We had no history other than my directing the church's small group ministry. This would be a challenge! How much easier it is to start a small group with at least a few people you know. On the flip side, what a wonderful challenge and opportunity it is to be part of a new group of young people eager to be challenged in their faith. With this in mind, I was excited and anxious to get to know this gathered, diverse group of young people, and for them to get to know one another.

In a newly formed group, it is always a wise idea to start with the process of self-disclosure, so I asked a very safe question, "Where did you grow up and what made that place interesting?" Surely everyone could answer that. Then we moved on to "How long have you lived in the Boston area? "What brought you here?" Next I asked, " What one thing would you really like to see happen in this new small group, and what would make this group worth your attending?" And so we began our journey. Eventually we named ourselves the "Awesome Group" and for our two years together, it was a perfect description.

CREATING EFFECTIVE DISCUSSION

Asking a good question is the key to creating meaningful discussion. It assists in the self-disclosure aspect of group life and eventually becomes a pow- erful tool for accountability. Well-constructed questions help the members of the group discover biblical truths for themselves. It is therefore important that the leader cultivate the ability to ask the right question at the appropriate time. These questions become the springboard for discussion and help the group members make new discoveries about the Scripture and the implications for life and practice in the Christian faith. Later in this chapter I will provide solid, practical advice for constructing questions in general.

There are various types of questions that should be included in your group discussion. When constructing effective questions, it is essential for the leader to understand the important stages of growth each group can and should experience, as an effective question becomes the tool which drives the group through these differing stages. For instance, the above examples of sharing questions I asked my new small group are appropriate, simple, and safe ques- tions that begin the getting to know you process of the small group experience. As groups increase their knowledge of one another, trust levels during self-dis- closure rise and effective questions can include more personal risk. Therefore, in order to understand the foundation of what makes an effective question, it is necessary to explore the characteristics of the various stages of growth a group experiences over a period of time. These characteristics enable the leader to construct more appropriate sharing questions for self-disclosure and text questions for information sharing.

STAGES OF GROUP GROWTH

THE FOUR STAGES OF GROWTH FOR SMALL GROUPS

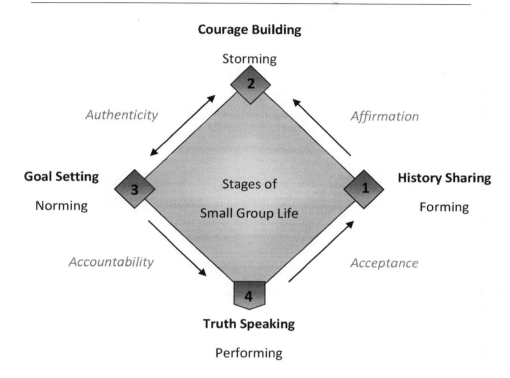

As we think about asking the good question, it is necessary to understand the various stages of life that groups experience while spending time together. Not until the leader understands the level of comfort and the existing individual mindsets can appropriate questions be constructed. The stages of group growth are known by various names that help us understand more vividly what is happening. For instance, the terms birth, infant, adolescent, and teenager help you visualize the various levels of maturity. Using the terms forming, storming, norming, and performing,[67] might induce a different concept of action, yet the big picture of creating a healthy environment for the growing trust level remains the same. In each description, the idea of progression and perhaps difficulty is implied. Whatever term is used (I will refer to stages as forming, storming, norming and performing), including the progression from history sharing, courage building, goal setting, and truth telling continue to

---

67 Roberta Hestenes, "Building Community through Small Groups," seminary course, Fuller Seminary, 1994. Much of my small group philosophy and understanding is based on information learned and experienced in this course. The stages of growth were described by these terms.

depict well-defined stages of healthy small group process. For a graphic illustration, the baseball diamond works perfectly.[68]

THE SHARING QUESTION

Sharing questions assist the getting to know you process. The sharing question becomes an effective way to build relationships and trust levels as the small group travels around the bases of small group life. We all have a story to tell. If thoughtful questions are asked, group members share more of their lives, trust levels rise, risks are taken, truth is told, and life-transformation can happen. They help everyone learn more about the members' lives, their interests, their challenges, and expectations. Sometimes the term for these questions is fire-starter or ice-breaker.

The purpose of the question is to begin to engage group members in comfortable sharing about themselves and their faith. It helps the group to warm up to one another, to interact with Scripture being discussed, and eventually to lead into appropriate accountability questions. When constructed thoughtfully and used wisely, the sharing question becomes strategic in the anticipated discussion for the evening.

STAGE 1: HISTORY SHARING

When a new small group is formed, ten to twelve people appear eager to start this spiritual journey as a team. Smiling faces and enthusiastic responses tend to portray a group of happy, well-adjusted participants. Yet, are they? Everyone wears a mask from time to time. This newly formed group is no different. At first glance everyone displays an expression of "I'm doing just fine," yet beneath this mask there may be lives struggling with depression, sense of failure, insecurity, and even thoughts of suicide. Stage one, the forming stage, is the beginning process of self-disclosure and discovery; it is a time to begin the development of trust and freedom that eventually reveals the hurts and disappointments each member experiences.

History sharing is an important stage of group life; it helps group members learn about their new circle of friends. It is a time of asking safe questions that

---

68 Lyman Coleman, Founder, Seredipity House, has used the baseball diamond to demonstrate stages of growth in small groups for many years. This useful graphic reinforces the importance of healthy group process. The diamond has been modified and the titles changed from the original.

encourage group members to tell their life stories. The sharing question, the getting to know you process, is important for hearing about past experiences of group members as they share their stories. Interesting connections begin to form. For instance, when asking the question, "Where did you grow up and what did you like about that place?" a group member might answer, "I spent most of my childhood on the south shore of Massachusetts. I loved being near the water and spending time on the ocean." Another group member might have had a similar experience or interest and now there is a connection and a relationship has begun to form.

The journey to first base (see graphic on page 135) is an opportunity to share safe, personal history and begin the process of moving on to present situations. "How long have you lived in Boston, and what brought you here?" reveals present involvements and discloses interests in either family, area of work, or education. In getting to know one another, safety is critical for getting off to a strong start. If an inappropriate sharing question of high risk is asked too early in the life of the group, fear and caution surface and trust is slow to develop. For instance, if I stated that we all should have the goal of spiritual growth and proceeded to ask "What is the most difficult sin you are struggling with at the moment?" I would probably be sitting alone in the group the following week!

In each stage of group life, the participants experience various emotions and expectations.[69] During Stage One, the personal history sharing phase, an atmosphere of acceptance is anticipated. Concerns might include:

» Will I feel accepted in this group?
» Will I like this group?
» Will this group like me?
» Can I trust this group when I talk about personal issues?
» What kind of commitment am I making to this group?
» How will I relate to the leader of this group?

In this phase of group life, the leader of the group should use the

---

69 Steve Barker, Johnson, Long, Malone, Nicholas., Small Group Leaders' Handbook (Downers Grove: InterVarsity Press, 1982), 49,54,57. Judy Johnson describes the dynamics of the four stages concerning the members and leaders. These charts are informative and useful in understanding group process. The original dynamics have been modified for my purposes.

authoritative (leader initiated) style of leadership. Being intentional about the leadership style and choosing appropriate sharing questions, help the group members feel comfortable and informed. This stage should continue for approximately six weeks of meetings. (Unfortunately, many small groups never move past first base and remain in a superficial relationship with one another for the duration of their small group experience.) It is here that the proper use of a well-constructed sharing question becomes a significant tool for moving group members around the next three bases.

Sharing questions might include:
» Where did you live when you were twelve and what did you like about it?
» When you were a teenager, what was your favorite room in your house?
» Have you had a really exciting vacation? If so, what did you do?
» What was one of the strangest jobs you ever had?

STAGE 2: COURAGE BUILDING

After the first six weeks or so the group should begin getting to know one another at a deeper level. Affirmation becomes part of the process. As the journey continues on to second base, masks are beginning to come off and group members should be experiencing a developing level of trust. However, if the group has been open to new people on a continuous basis, this trust level is slower to develop and may briefly regress into the first stage of acceptance.

The second stage, the storming stage, is the response to the developing level of comfort. During this time, the leader needs to move into the democratic (group initiated) style of leadership. Becoming more confident and comfortable, group members should take some ownership and begin to feel they are important to the life of the group. In this stage of courage building, "speaking the truth in love" (Ephesians 4:15) will start developing, and being frank and honest will be easier and more natural. The normal occurrence of conflict might result in this atmosphere of acceptance and affirmation, thus the name storming stage. The following describes the dynamics of this stage of growth:

» Members begin to take their relationship with one another seriously.
» They feel the leader cares for and respects them.
» Ownership has developed and the members become more engaged.
» The group becomes "our group" opposed to "Tom's group."

» The group will start meeting some of the needs of its members.
» Members start to take risks with their self-disclosure.

Leaders need to be aware of the possibility of conflict in this stage. Conflict is normal and can be advantageous. (Our next chapter will help you through the process of resolving conflict in a way that honors God.) Frustrations about group life or particular personalities often surface. It is also in this stage where the group leader occasionally feels threatened in his or her leadership role. When people begin to discover their spiritual gifts, and inwardly believe "I could lead this group!" tension can arise. Delegating responsibilities for the group meeting assists in positively developing the spiritual gifts represented in the group members and is important for developing future small group leaders.

In this stage, sharing questions move from the past experiences to present situations. Questions involve more risk and might include the following:

» What do you do on a typical Wednesday?
» What is a good thing happening in your life right now? What makes it good?
» What task do you have to do this week that is difficult for you? Why is it difficult?
» In what way is this small group an encouragement to you?
» In what way can we improve the developing relationships in this group?

STAGE 3: GOAL SETTING

As trust levels become stronger, group members move into a more confident relationship with other group members. Rounding second base and heading into third, the group begins to reach maturity and authenticity. This stage, the norming stage, realizes that the small group has taken on a life of its own, goals are being met, and relationships with one another and God are growing deeper. The attributes of knowing, loving, serving, admonishing, and celebrating are being experienced. Members begin to be more open and honest when discussing the personal tensions of integrating faith and practice in a pluralistic world. Some of the accompanying dynamics might include:

» Members' masks are being removed because they feel accepted.
» Because the environment is safe and comfortable, members feel free to talk openly about private areas of their lives.

» Group goals begin to be accomplished; more focus on mission.
» Role of discussion leader is shared and members' spiritual gifts utilized.

Leaders need to be aware of the various emerging strengths and gift-edness of group members. Allowing others to be the discussion leader or prayer leader will help members to consider and be excited about their own future leadership. A group can continue in this stage for many weeks as long as the group includes mission and creative outreach. Otherwise, the group will become ingrown and ineffective. A group that stays together for a long period of time with no goals for reaching outside the confines of the immediate group becomes unhealthy.

In this Goal Setting stage, sharing questions begin to include more risk in vulnerability in order to move the group into deeper self-disclosure and accountability. Previously set goals for the group are evaluated and new goals expressed. Examples of sharing questions might include:

» Think of a time when you felt abandoned by God. Briefly describe your feelings.
» What is one area of struggle in your Christian faith? In what way can our small group help you?
» What is one change that you would like to make in your life? Why is that important?
» If you could wave a magic wand that would make your job (marriage, family, church, friendship) perfect, name one or two changes that would be made. What one step can you take this week to help make that change begin to happen?

STAGE 4: TRUTH TELLING

Accountability has been established and authentic Christian community has been experienced in the small group. This stage, the performing stage, begins the process of asking "Where do we go from here?" The small group has experienced love, spiritual growth, group confession, prayer, and healing through God's empowering Spirit. Mission has been an important ingredient of the small group life. Goals have been reached, the covenant has been reshaped several times, and group termination becomes an issue of discussion.

Most likely the thought of multiplying the group will not be popular as the members have enjoyed one another and the routine is comfortable. Group multiplication, however, needs to happen in order to involve more people with on-going community care and connection. Since members have enjoyed sharing their spiritual journeys, they will want their familiar routine to continue. Termination becomes a challenge. Part of the process of ending well involves honest evaluation of each member's experience and future anticipations. Evaluation questions that assist in group closure might include some of the following reflections:

» Was it worth it? Why or why not?
» What did I learn about God, myself, others?
» This experience has been a strong motivation for growing spiritually. What steps will I take to be part of another small group for care and connection?
» I am thankful for my group of fellow travelers. In what way can we support each other in the future?

Small group leaders need to return to the authoritative (leader initiated) style of leadership in order to help the small group transition and end well. Consider the following suggestions:

» Discuss the group ending time well in advance. It should be stated in the covenant.
» Make the ending pleasant for everyone. Recognize that it is hard to say "good-bye" so honor and encourage one another.
» Suggest each member share appreciation for one another and celebrate what God has done in and through your group. Have a party!
» Encourage and enable group members to join new groups or start their own.

The small group cycle has been completed. The group has moved through history sharing and acceptance; courage building and affirmation; goal setting and authenticity; and finally, truth speaking and accountability. If the group does not multiply but invites several new people into the group or changes the focus of the group's purpose, the new group will start the journey around the bases once again.

CHARACTERISTICS OF A GOOD QUESTION

Jesus asked very powerful, significant questions when interacting with others. He always made them think for themselves and caused them to examine their hearts. A good question is key to maintaining thought-provoking dialogue. Leaders need to consider what makes a good question and utilize them in the group discussion. It is through these questions small group members discover biblical truths for themselves. Good questions are valuable because they help the leader evaluate the members' understanding of the Bible, cause the members to think through the issue at hand, and help prevent the leader from becoming the autocratic leader who spends too much time lecturing from his or her own knowledge. The goal of questions is twofold: to help the small group members share their life stories and respond to the text of focus.

"As a rule of thumb, discussion questions usually look for information members of the group have but the leader my not have."[70] This simple and good advice is worth remembering as we plan our approach for the group discussion. The goal of the small group leader is not to be continually giving out information he or she has learned, but to involve group members in meaningful discussion about the text studied. It is general knowledge that, after a month, individuals retain only 10 percent of what they have heard. A subject that is listened to and interacted with through the use of effective questions and discussions causes the retention to rise to 80-90 percent. This statistic should motivate a leader to pay attention to the value of a good question in creating a healthy and meaningful group dialogue.

As Jesus caused people to think for themselves and examine their hearts, a leader must do the same in order to keep advancing around the bases of group life. Whether the question is a sharing question for self-disclosure or a question of the text for information, there are several practical suggestions in creating an engaging discussion.

1. Ask questions that call for information that is new to others in the group: "If you had a free day, where would you go and what would you do?" The group member has an opportunity for story telling that helps to let others know favorite places, hobbies or activities. It becomes the getting to know you part of building relationships. Questions of this kind are appropriate for the forming stage of the small group.

---

70 Karen Lee-Thorp, How To Ask Great Questions (Colorado Springs: NavPress, 1998), 7. This is an excellent short work on guiding your group to discovery.

2. Ask a question that has valuable information. Instead of asking "What is your favorite food?" ask "If you were stuck on an island and could have one item of food with you, what would you choose?" This is a more interesting way of finding out little details about peoples' lives during the forming stage of group life. I used this question in a seeker group one week and a young woman expressed a love for dark chocolate. It was apparent to me that she was initially very uneasy with the group experience and I suspected she was not going to return the following week. While visiting my daughter and her family the following weekend, their baby sitter, who was selling candy bars for a fundraiser, stopped by. I bought a huge dark chocolate bar and brought it to our next seeker meeting hoping she would return. She did. As I slid the candy bar across the table to her, her eyes became amazingly big. The fact that I had remembered and bought her the candy became a simple bond between the two of us. She continued to attend the group and eventually placed her faith in Jesus Christ. Now, obviously it was not just the chocolate bar but the care and attention which most likely helped her feel comfortable in the group.

3. Try to avoid superlatives. Asking "What is the worst experience you have ever had?" will cause confusion as people want to make sure they have picked the right experience. Choosing words like worst, best, most favorite, suggest only one answer and usually cause people to think later of a better example. And, when they make their decision, it is difficult to keep the discussion brief. A better question would be phrased, "Briefly share one exciting moment you experienced this year. What made the moment exciting?" or "Who has been a significant influence in your spiritual life. Why?"

4. Be careful not to ask a question that is too risky or revealing when the group is in the forming stage. Asking questions that require members to make confessions or reveal information about their lives too soon in the getting to know you stage of life is uncomfortable for most people. Instead of asking "What sin are you really struggling with at the moment?" you might ask "Briefly describe one or two temptations you are experiencing in the marketplace (family, relationships, finances) that challenge you in your faith?" This type question is appropriate for the storming and norming stage of group life.

143

5. Ask questions that everyone can answer. Asking "What college did you attend?" or "How did you meet your husband?" can be embarrassing or difficult for the person who did not go to college or who is not married. Until a leader knows the group's background well, a better question might be "Where did you learn the trade that you find yourself employed in at the moment?" The meeting a spouse question should wait until the group knows each other better. However, it would be a wonderful early sharing question for a married couples group.

6. Be careful not to ask more than two questions at once (unless they are written). Most people remember one or two, but will always ask for the third question to be repeated. Instead of asking "Where did you live when you were twelve?" "What did you like about that place?" and "What is your most favorite memory?" ask "Think about where you lived when you were twelve. What comes to mind as one of the favorite things you liked to do?" People often will give some context to the answer by saying, "Well, I lived in the mid-west and loved hiking the mountains."

7. Be careful not to use closed ended questions. When you ask a group, "Did you get anything out the Scripture we studied this week?" you will have two options for an answer: "Yes" or "No". End of discussion! If you ask a closed ended question, follow it up with an open ended question such as "If so, what was one challenge?" or "In what way?" Following up a closed ended question with "Why?" can be effective if the leader does not create the atmosphere that challenges the member with his or her reasoning. In the performing stage of group life, use a follow-up question that is useful for creating accountability with one another.

8. Questions requiring only a single answer are not very stimulating. Instead of asking "Who is the speaker?" say "Talk about the characters involved in this conversation. How are they interacting with Jesus?" A question that requires an answer concerning location or a particular event could be stated "What do you know about foot-washing in that culture?" or "Briefly explain what you know about the Decapolis." To increase the self-disclosure and create more accountability you might ask "Put yourself in the text setting. What emotions would Jesus have invoked in you by saying what he said? Why?"

9. Do not ask questions that constantly focus on group members' apparent problems. Mix up your questions so people can share problems, yet have opportunities to celebrate their victories. As the group travels around the bases of group life, members will become more comfortable and more vulnerable with honest sharing concerning personal struggles. Asking questions that allow for a time of honoring God are exhilarating, so do not forget to include them.

10. Do not expect the group to enjoy going around the circle for answers. It causes people to think about how they might respond rather than paying attention to what is being shared. Create an environment where group members can enter into the discussion in a spontaneous manner. Group members tend to be less engaged when they are assigned a question and most often prefer to have a choice.

Following these guidelines will create better dialogue. When asking questions, particularly sharing questions, it is important for the leader to set the example that models specifics, vulnerability, and length of time for the responses. (Group members also need to be reminded that the leader has weaknesses and needs.) If you have a group of twelve people and expect everyone to share, unless you are careful, you will spend far too much time on one question. Not everyone needs to respond to questions asked. The leader needs to know when to move the conversation along so as to complete the study on time. You may have to interject that important word briefly in your question by saying "Let's keep our answers brief and hear from a few of you."

SAMPLE QUESTIONS TO EVALUATE

In summary and in response to the above suggestions, look at the following questions. Which questions are effective and why? Which questions should be reworded and for what reason? Be prepared to discuss your decisions at your next small group meeting.

1. What are the areas of life where you feel like a failure?
2. In what area of your spiritual life do you know God is displeased?
3. What is your favorite color?
4. When you have free time, how do you like to spend it?
5. Describe your most significant learning experience.
6. When did you start attending this church and what attracted you?

7. What is one thing you like about our church and one thing you would like to see improved?
8. What things have you worried about the most this week?
9. What five steps can you take this week to restore your relationship with your boss?
10. In what way did you resonate with the characters in this text?

EXAMPLES OF SHARING QUESTIONS

The following questions are examples of sharing questions that start at a safe, superficial level and progress to a more self-revealing, risk-taking level. Think carefully about appropriate sharing questions as your group is being formed. If you need help, here are several resources available for helping you think through constructing sharing questions.[71]

» What is a favorite place in your home or apartment? Briefly describe.
» When you have free time, what do you like to do?
» If you received one unexpected present, what would you like it to be?
» What is one place in the world you would like to visit? Why?
» When do you remember hearing about Jesus and what did you think about him?
» If you could pick one character in fiction, movies or television, who would that be? Briefly describe the reason for your choice.
» What is one thing you worried about this week? One thing that gave you joy?
» What is a significant need in your life at the moment? In what way can our small group help?
» What one area of your life is hard to give over to God? Why?

LOGGING IN: A SHARING TECHNIQUE

When the small group is experiencing relational maturity in faith reflection, a short-cut sharing technique called Logging In is helpful. This process allows each group member to raise their own agenda for sharing and personal reflection. Rather than have group members respond to one or two faith sharing questions, the leader simply asks each member to bring the group up-to-date

---

71 Steve Sheely, Small Group Ice-Breakers and Heart-Warmers (Nashville: Serendipity House, 1996) and Jerry D. Jones, 201 Great Questions for Married Couples (Colorado Springs: NavPress, 1999) are examples of sharing questions resources available in Christian bookstores or online sites.

with what his or her current and important faith issues are. Each person initiates the topic and depth of their own sharing. Group interaction allows questions for the clarity of the situation, encouragement, or celebration. This becomes a wonderful tool for implementing accountability into the group.

OPEN-ENDED SHARING

Be creative and vary your sharing time. An alternate to Logging-In is to use an open-ended sentence in a short, incomplete form. Questions can be asked by the leader encouraging group members to finish the sentence. This process is less threatening than Logging In, but still allows truth speaking and vulnerability. Some examples include:

- » I was frustrated this week about . . .
- » A person who touched my life was . . .
- » Some theological thoughts I've had are . . .
- » A high point for my family was . . .
- » A low point for me was . . .
- » My week at home (or work) was . . .

WRITING A BIBLE STUDY

SHARING QUESTIONS

When introducing the text for the Bible study, asking sharing questions structured around the theme of the study is an effective way to enter into the Bible discussion. Biblical sharing questions become natural segues into the text for the group study; they help to get members thinking personally about the Scripture and what it implies in their lives.

If you are studying prayer, you might ask "What was the first type of prayer that you remember praying?" or "When is it difficult for you to pray?" If you are studying marketplace ethics, you might ask "What is one challenge you face in the workplace? In what way does your faith help or hinder?" If you are studying about forgiveness you might ask "Think of a time when you asked forgiveness from someone. What made it difficult?" If you are leading a short-term task group, ask "What gets you excited about being part of this group? What are some of your concerns?" All of these examples help to move a newly formed group into self-disclosure that creates a trusting arena as you start your in-depth study of the text or undertake a particular task.

If Luke chapter 15 is the focus of the study, various themes can be emphasized by asking sharing questions relating to being lost, forgiven, restored, or being jealous. In the Luke 15:11-32 text (the prodigal son) a couple of sharing questions might be:

> » Have you ever run away from home? If so, and if you feel comfortable, share the situation with the group.
> » Think of a time when you were totally lost. What emotions did you experience?

The leader has now set the scene for discussing running away and being lost. Thus, there have been personal stories shared, perhaps a bit of laughter or even an expression of an unhappy time of life, but the group becomes more focused on what Jesus has to say about being spiritually lost. There is significant value in using the well-constructed sharing question as an introduction to your Bible study. The leader should keep in mind the stage of growth of the small group and construct either a past, present, or future type sharing question that relates to the theme of the study.

TEXT QUESTIONS

As discussed in the last chapter, lesson preparation, there are important questions of the text that need to be asked: "What do I observe?" "How should I interpret this text?" and "In what way will I apply this information into my life?" At the end of each chapter in this book, you have participated in a Bible study. The questions model the observation, interpretation, and application format and move from safe questions to more risky, self-disclosure. Although small group leaders often prefer to use guidebooks with prepared questions, there is value in the discussion leader understanding the process of how to turn observation, interpretation, and application material into effective questions. Being able to form good questions not only helps with the evaluation process for guidebook consideration, but is instructive for those who wish to use only the Bible during their time together. Using the Bible and working through the text by asking good questions is challenging and can be a strong method for studying the Scripture.[72]

---

72 Roberta Hestenes, Using the Bible in Groups (Philadelphia: The Westminster Press, 1983). This is an excellent resource for using only the Bible during your study time. Many study ideas are presented.

OBSERVATION QUESTIONS

In studying the Scripture the, who, what, where, when, why and how questions are asked. You will want your group to discuss the important observations of the text, so be sure to turn your observation material into questions appropriate for the life stage of the small group. Considering the Luke 15:11-32 passage, some observation questions might include:

» Who are the main characters in the text? Briefly describe.
» Where does this take place? What is the family situation?
» Are there significant words and places you discovered about the text? If so, briefly describe.
» How did the characters involved respond to the father's forgiveness?

INTERPRETATION QUESTIONS

After having observed the facts of the Scripture, your goal is to seek the meaning and significance of those facts. Turning your interpretation ideas into questions leads the group into understanding the author's purpose for writing the passage. Let the group discuss their point of views, but remember the key to interpretation is finding the reason the author had for writing the passage. If the final interpretation is different from what the author intended, it is not a good interpretation. Interpretation questions might include:

» What did Luke want the readers to hear?
» Does this text describe God? If so, in what way?
» Why does Jesus describe how the older brother responded?
» What is the point of this text? What does Jesus want us to learn about sin, God's love and His forgiveness?

APPLICATION QUESTIONS

The application questions are the so what? and now what? questions. If the leader does not work through the lesson in a timely manner, the challenge for what group members will do differently because they studied the particular text is omitted. It is critical that the Bible study end with personal application. The group should be challenged to see how their attitudes, relationships, and actions need to be changed. Rather than making a final statement for what everyone should have learned, ask effective application questions that create stronger mind impressions and heart-felt responses. Examples might include:

>> Think about one area in your life that is a challenge. In what way are you running from God concerning this issue?
>> Briefly describe a time when you felt you were running into the loving arms of God, your Father. What were some of your emotions?
>> Do you identify more with the younger brother or the elder brother? Why?
>> What one step can you take this week to rest in the arms of God's forgiving love?

"The Word of God holds up a mirror in which we can see our own face: our character, values, attitudes, and habits. It offers us a perspective on our situation and relationships that we can't get on our own. At the same time, it opens up a window into the realm of God, a window in which we see the face of Christ looking back at us. We get to compare our face to that of Christ, noting the similarities and differences."[73]

Spending sufficient time with the application questions challenges each group member to look into the mirror God's Word holds before them. Until we are open to the life-transforming truth of Scripture and apply the lessons into our daily lives, our Bible study is just a time of collecting information. With effective application questions, the leader helps the group members mature in their spiritual journey.

As you become more familiar with constructing effective questions, you can combine observation and interpretation questions. Use the opportunity to ask an application question early within the text and challenge the group members with their response. Again, you need to remember the stage of growth of your group and ask appropriate questions that do not threaten the self-disclosure process. The leader does, however, need to take a risk at the right time in order to keep the group trust level advancing from superficial sharing.

Think again about the negative environment you may have experienced in a small group setting. Perhaps the discussion was just boring. Thinking about what makes a good question and planning wisely for effective discussion will make the small group experience exciting and worth the group's commitment.

---

73 Lee-Thorp, 55.

The goal is to get the members talking to one another by creating healthy inter-action. A thoughtful, effective question will do this.

As the leader asks the appropriate question, paying attention to creating inclusive dialogue among the group members is important. At first the group members will address the leader directly. As the group starts the bonding pro-cess, the leader needs to use his or hers communication skills to encourage all group members to share. The leader must not dominate the discussion or answer all the questions asked by the members. Leaders also need to be com-fortable with some silence (as people are thinking) and be careful not to appear impatient by answering the questions they have asked. If there is prolonged silence, rephrase the question and wait until people respond.

THOUGHT PROVOKING QUESTIONS

1. DISCUSS

Asking effective questions are important for the vitality of your group discussion. Discuss new ideas you learned concerning the value of constructing good, effective questions and their relationship to the small group's stage of growth. Review and share your answers to the list of sample questions given for you to evaluate.

The Bible study for this chapter is to be constructed by you as part of the leader training preparation. Read the Scripture, collect pertinent information by asking the important questions of the text, and construct appropriate questions for the stage and trust level of your leadership training small group friends. Share and evaluate your questions with one another.

THE QUESTION OF IDENTITY
Mark 2:1-12

2. TELL

Construct two appropriate sharing questions that pertain to the theme of this Scripture.

3. SCRIPTURE

Briefly state the context of the text and ask a volunteer to read Mark 2:1-12.

Look (observation) What do you want your group to discover concerning the who, what, where, when, why, or how information? Construct two appropriate questions.

Think (interpretation) What questions are important for determining the purpose and meaning of the text? Construct two appropriate questions (why and how question might be helpful.)

Act (application) What challenges would you like your small group to consider and act upon in response to the study of this portion of Scripture? Construct two appropriate questions.

4. PRAYER

Take a few moments to pray about your responses concerning the challenge Jesus has given throughout the Mark 2:1-12 text. Share prayer requests and pray for one another using the conversational method of prayer.

5. PREPARATION

Select the discussion leader for your next meeting together. Complete the next Bible study on difficult personalities and conflict resolution. Pray for one another throughout the week.

"I am the way and the truth and the life.
No one comes to the Father except through me.
If you really knew me, you would know my Father as well.
From now on, you do know him and have seen him."

John 14:6

TROUBLESHOOTING: CONFLICT RESOLUTION

"Conflict is not undesirable. It is of the very essence of life within a community that values difference and honors the diversity of God's creative design evidenced in humanity."

Sam Portaro, *Conflict and a Christian Life*

Conflict happens. Conflict is important in the growing dynamics of authentic small group life and community. It is probably safe to assume that we all have, at some point, grieved over controversy and the consequences of the experience. Perhaps you are already recalling a situation of conflict that was disappointing, painful, and damaging. Being perceptive and knowing the tools for conflict resolution curbs much of the destructive consequences that need not happen.

Early on in my life of ministry I experienced an extremely stressful situation that ultimately taught me many lessons on conflict and leadership. With a good friend, together we had started a Bible study ministry. The enrollment was almost overwhelming. The responsibilities of management were mounting. Within a short period of time, however, it was evident that we possessed totally different and conflicting styles of leadership. Frustration increased and the friendship was threatened. How does one preserve the quality of ministry, value existing friendships, yet create an environment where both parties can fully utilize their spiritual gifts?

As a task driven person who liked to think of herself as a perfectionist, I planned well in advance and had certain expectations of people involved in the same adventure. My friend, on the other hand, sent a strong message of lack of trust by the inability or desire to delegate, while taking on more responsibility than she could handle well. Much of the implementation of the newly formed ministry was done at the last minute. It created frustration and tension while driving a wedge into our long, meaningful friendship.

The controversy was becoming destructive. With the fragility of our relationship, both of us knew confrontation was in order. We acted on what we thought would be the healthiest options for resolution. Personalities and leadership styles were probably not going to change quickly, if at all. Unrealized expectations and the unexpressed hurtful feelings needed to be verbalized if reconciliation was to happen. The relationship was guarded. It would have been easier to quit and do something else. But, knowing that it would please God and for the benefit of the thriving ministry, we worked through various perceptions and responses to each other's leadership styles.

We decided to pray weekly with one another for the restoration of this long-lived friendship. It was hard, but it was significant. God blessed our time together and gradually we sorted out our responsibilities with appropriate time schedules. The relationship was slowly salvaged. The experience taught an important lesson; often it is not the conflict that ruins a relationship, but the lack of understanding how to correctly process the subject of the conflict.

Conflict happens between individuals and within groups. For most people, conflict is uncomfortable, yet some people find it quite delightful. When a small group forms and attempts to make decisions, conflict will surface. "In almost every meeting room within every organization, people are disagreeing with each other. Whether the organization is a business, an industry, a government agency, a hospital, a school, a law firm, church group (emphasis added), or a family, disagreements occur as decisions are made and problems are solved. Involved participation in such situations means that different ideas, opinions, beliefs, and information will surface and clash. The result is controversy—the conflict that arises when one person's ideas, information, conclusions, theories, and opinions are incompatible with those of another person, and the two seek to reach an agreement."[74]

This type of controversy has potential for being part of the healthy growth of the group as a whole and individually for each member. Conflict is natural to any group gathering where relational intimacy is desired. If it does not happen, chances are the group has not taken risks for challenging one another to achieve authentic community. Conflict can be a healthy dynamic. Leaders need to expect conflict to surface, yet at the same time, have a responsibility to know how to deal correctly with conflict and make sure it does not lend itself to group destruction.

According to Webster's dictionary, the root of the word conflict means "together strike." Together we strike at one another through disagreements of ideas and interests, we clash with different personalities, leadership styles, and we cause emotional disturbances while clinging to the personal hopes and expectations of life in general. The element of fear and the threat of change put us on the defensive, driving the desire to ignore or run from the problematic situation. However the conflict is managed, it is always challenging and often painful.

When conflict develops and is managed properly, those involved learn valuable lessons about themselves and others. God uses conflict to grow us spiritually. And if we think that conflict has no place in the lives of God's children, we need to look more closely at Scripture and see the many situations of conflict throughout the lives of God's people. For instance, we can begin in Genesis in the Garden of Eden; the conflict of choice. Later we see conflict of jealousy in the life of Cain resulting in the death of Abel; in the longstanding jealousy between Jacob and Esau in the theft of the birthright; contempt for Moses with the years in the wilderness; material possessions and land occupation obscuring the plan of God; rejection of God's will for personal desires at the expense of murder, and the conflicts of war and acts of violence voiced in the writings of the prophets, and eventually in the developing church of new believers.

Jesus was a master of creating conflict purely on the basis of who he claimed to be. There were times when he purposely asked questions that often resulted in conflict. This became a tool for Jesus to develop personal consideration for

---

74 David W. Johnson and Frank P. Johnson, Joining Together: Group Theory and Group Skills, 4th ed., (Boston: Allyn and Bacon, 1991), 259.

what the kingdom of God represented. There were situations of conflict within the group of disciples as to who was the most loved; conflict in being willing to support and be identified as a follower; conflict with the most efficient use of the disciples' purse; and conflict with how and with whom Jesus would spend his time. And it was the developing conflict and threatening consequences that eventually took Jesus' life. So at the heart of conflict is ultimately who is in control and who will prevail.

> Conflict has been part of the life of God's people from the earliest intimations of their relationship with God. Within the imaginative explorations into human origins and experiences, the rich stories of human and historical relationships, and the poetic utterances to a God who is gradually revealed, as each of us is to the other -- in the daily unfolding of life—we see that difference and conflict are essential, inevitable components of being. They are as necessary to our life as water, fire and air. And like these powerful elements, whose various combinations and admixtures can mean either life or death for us, difference and conflict demand our respect. They have the power to sustain life, and to destroy it.[75]

Conflict, therefore, is common in small group settings. Often it stems from a lack of understanding and expectations of the group. When groups do not intentionally design the goals and purposes of their group life, there is no foundation for vision and evaluation. As people grow spiritually and are stretched through taking risks with their sharing, new dynamics are created. Member's expectations vary in their comfort level and conflict often surfaces.

Conflict occurs with inappropriate leadership styles. When leaders are not sensitive to the stage of life of the group or willing to delegate and give ownership for group development, members get edgy and confrontation surfaces.

Every small group is diverse in personalities. There's a popular saying that "porcupines far off look cute and cuddly; at close range, however, they are quite prickly!" So it is with the various members of the small group when self-disclosure happens and relationships develop. Some personalities are helpful characteristics in small group life and others create detrimental tendencies. As we consider conflict and how to manage the experience in the small group, it is worth taking time to first consider the various responses we own or experience

---

75   Sam Portaro, Conflict and a Christian Life (Cambridge, Massachusetts: Cowley Publications, 2003), 26.

in conflict situations. Considering various options for conflict management and resolution becomes necessary for healthy small group life and useful with the personalities you might encounter as you lead your small group.

As we consider reactions to controversy, how do you respond when conflict presents itself? Think about how your family handled conflict when you were young. In what way have you adopted the model you experienced in your early years? Perhaps you are thinking about some common responses: "Just ignore it," "it's just the way she is," "you're right so forget it," "just move on," and perhaps "do unto others before they do it unto you!" We all have been trained through various experiences at a young age and these instances could influence how we respond when conflict within our present sphere of relationships occurs. More often than not, conflict is seen as a win-lose situation that is destructive and is to be avoided at all cost. In actuality, it is the method of dealing with the conflict that taints our perception of how conflict, when managed properly, can be used to great advantage.

SIX GENERALIZATIONS THAT SHAPE AND REINFORCE CONFLICT PERCEPTIONS:

1. Harmony is normal; conflict is abnormal.
2. Conflict is always a win-lose situation; someone will be a winner and someone a loser.
3. Conflict is the natural result of personality clashes.
4. All conflict is wrong.
5. Christians must never conflict, but are commanded to live in conformity.
6. The Christian way to handle conflict is to give in, esteeming the other out of Christian love.[76]

FIVE ALTERNATIVE RESPONSES IN CONFLICT SITUATIONS:

1. "I win—you lose"
2. "I want out, I'll withdraw"
3. "I'll give in for good relations"
4. "I'll meet you halfway"
5. "I can care and confront"[77]

---

76 Julie Gorman, Community That Is Christian (Wheaton: Victor Books, 1993), 192-193.
77 David Augsburger, Caring Enough To Confront (Ventura: Regal Books, 1981), 13.

There are differing styles when dealing with conflict that often are influenced either by circumstances or personalities. Often people recoil and avoid conflict at all cost, others attack, some become condescending, and another compromises to make peace. Small group leaders need to be perceptive as conflict begins to happen. Immediate attention to the dynamics helps to lessen the intensity when group life is challenged. If leaders ignore a developing problem, or over exercise management tools, future conflict may be suppressed and the freedom of expression or the developing conflict may not surface for healthy attention. When this happens, groups do not bond, trust is not developed, and members drop out with frustration commenting that the group just didn't work.

> Life without confrontation is directionless, aimless, passive. When unchallenged, human beings tend to drift, to wander, or to stagnate. Confrontation is a gift. Confrontation is a necessary stimulation to jog one out of mediocrity or to prod one back from extremes. Confrontation is an art to be learned.[78]

Johnson and Johnson describe five basic strategies most common when dealing with conflict. For people who are visual, these images are extremely helpful in assisting with the process of resolution.

1. The Turtle (Withdrawing). Turtles withdraw into their shells to avoid conflicts. They give up their personal goals and relationships. They stay away from the issues over which the conflict is taking place and from the persons they are in conflict with. Turtles believe it is hopeless to try to resolve conflicts. They feel helpless. They believe it is easier to withdraw (physically and psychologically) from a conflict than to face it.

2. The Shark (Forcing). Sharks try to overpower opponents by forcing them to accept their solution to the conflict. Their goals are highly important to them, and relationships are of minor importance. They seek to achieve their goals at all costs. They are not concerned with the needs of others. They do not care if others like or accept them. Sharks assume that conflicts are settled by one person winning and one person losing. They want to be the winner. Winning gives sharks a sense of pride and achievement. Losing gives them a sense of weakness, inadequacy, and failure. They try to win by attacking, overpowering, overwhelming, and intimidating others.

---

78 Ibid., 51.

3. The Teddy Bear (Smoothing). To teddy bears the relationship is of great importance while their own goals are of little importance. Teddy bears want to be accepted and liked by others. They think that conflict should be avoided in favor of harmony and that people cannot discuss conflicts without damaging relationships. They are afraid that if the conflict continues, someone will get hurt, and that would ruin the relationship. They give up their goals to preserve the relationship. Teddy bears say, "I'll give up my goals and let you have what you want, in order for you to like me." Teddy bears try to smooth over the conflict out of fear of harming the relationship.

4. The Fox (Compromising). Foxes are moderately concerned with their own goals and their relationships with others. Foxes seek a compromise; they give up part of their goals and persuade the other person in a conflict to give up part of his goals. They seek a conflict solution in which both sides gain something—the middle ground between two extreme positions. They are willing to sacrifice part of their goals and relationships in order to find agreement for the common good.

5. The Owl (Confronting). Owls highly value their own goals and relationships. They view conflicts as problems to be solved and seek a solution that achieves both their own goals and the goals of the other person. Owls see conflict as a means of improving relationships by reducing tension between two persons. They try to begin a discussion that identifies the conflict as a problem. By seeking solutions that satisfy both themselves and the other person, owls maintain the relationship. Owls are not satisfied until a solution is found that achieves their own goals and the other person's goals. And they are not satisfied until the tensions and negative feelings have been fully resolved.[79]

To understand and recognize not only your strategy, but also the various strategies represented in your group, significantly enhances the ability of the group to move forward into resolution. It would be well-spent time in a group meeting to discover the various strategies the group member tends to utilize for when conflict arises (which it will) your group will be more wisely prepared for healthy resolution.

It is helpful for leaders to recognize their normal strategy of conflict resolution as it becomes very useful in diverse situations to switch to another strategy

---

79 Johnson and Johnson, 307-309.

depending on the circumstances and goals of the conflict. "Each conflict strategy, however, has its place. You do not want to be an overspecialized dinosaur who can deal with conflict in only one way. You need to be able to use any one of the five, depending on your goals and the relationship. In one conflict, you may wish to use one strategy, while in another conflict you may wish to use a different strategy. To be effective in resolving conflicts, you have to vary your actions according to what will work best in the situation. You need to be able to switch actions according to what will work best."[80]

The flexibility of strategies according to the situation becomes a helpful tool for reaching resolution rather than being frozen in stubborn mindsets. The turtle and the teddy bear, for instance, may alter the importance of high relationships for more focus on goals and the shark and the owl may have to alter their importance on goals and aim for the value of relationships. The fox, on the other hand, might have to make a more intentional commitment to either the relationship or the goal at hand.

WHEN AND HOW TO CONFRONT CONFLICT

As the small group travels around the bases of life together, conflict tends to surface when members begin to feel comfortable. Ownership has been developed and perhaps suddenly, or not so suddenly, one individual decides the leader or someone in the group is dispensable. Concepts and implementations of group life are challenged. As accountability begins to surface between group members, self-reliance and self-defense for particular beliefs or behaviors become barriers for harmony. Perhaps it's that annoying personality that one or two members can no longer tolerate. Whatever the reason or provocation, the leader needs to be astute in detecting a possible conflict. How and when we deal with it will determine the health and longevity of our group. Here are a few suggestions to keep in mind:

I. RECOGNITION

Identifying the presence of conflict is most essential. There's no use in pretending that it isn't happening, and it is not wise to think the group is a failure because it is happening. Never attack a member of the group with the title instigator verbally or with body language. Instead, think of caring responses

---

80 Ibid., 309.

such as: "I sense the rising of some anxiety here." "Am I correct in assuming this response triggered some anger in you?" "Can we identify what the core of the anger might be?" Particular feelings need to be heard and when they have been expressed, the leader can move on to the particulars. Asking a nebulous question such as "what are you feeling right now" is not a helpful question, so ask a question that enables identification of the source.

"Separate the people from the problems. Emotions typically become entangled with the objective merits of the problem. Taking positions just makes this worse because people's egos become identified with their positions. The participants should come to see themselves as working side by side, attacking the problem, not each other."[81] In identifying the source of conflict, make sure to separate the person from the problem. Identify the conflict.

2. PRAYER

Prayer for the conflict circumstances, the people involved, and the resolution sought, brings us before God with willing hearts to hear, act upon, and involve Him in the method of resolution. It is an important reminder for us to be continually praying for our group members. And remembering that conflict is often healthy and stimulating for spiritual growth, it becomes a time of celebration for what God has done in us and through us during the challenging and seemingly difficult time. Surround the process of conflict resolution in continual prayer.

3. ACTIVE LISTENING

When dealing with differing views concerning an action, belief, or behavior, listen reflectively. Allow one person to state how they see the problem through their lens without interruptions. Listen in the same manner to the second or third person involved in the conflict. If the issue appears muddy or not well verbalized, perhaps out of emotions or lack of understanding, clarify the remarks. The leader might say, "am I hearing you correctly when you say the problem originates with ...?" or "I am not sure I completely understand what the core problem is. Would you please restate for me what you just said?"

When there is an issue between two people, the leader might say, "John, would you please restate what you think Mike just said?" And, "Mike would you

---

81 Roger Fisher, William Ury and Bruce Patton, Getting to Yes; Negotiating Agreement Without Giving In, 2nd ed., (New York: Penguin Books, 1991), 10-11.

please restate what you think John was saying to you?" Individuals can easily get off track and caught up in emotions by hearing what they want to hear and not what was actually said. Many conflicts are easily resolved when parties understand that they have been misunderstood. On the other hand, more damaging conflicts need serious attention and may have to be resolved outside the confines of group life.

4. LOOK FOR AGREEMENT

Look for areas where both parties agree. Approach the areas of agreement first with an opening comment, "we all agree that there are times that conflict can occur in a healthy small group. An important commitment and agreement we all have made to this group is to respect each other's differences and honest input; we want to hear about them." Or "here is where I think both of you are in agreement." Now the focus is not on the differences allowing the leader to approach the prickly areas of disagreement or conflict. We have given permission for each person to take a risk and put words to the conflict at hand.

5. ACT ON COMPLAINTS

We all have experienced conflict with family, friends, or colleagues where responses reflect an honest attempt for change. "I will do things differently so you won't feel that way again," or "I understand your situation better and I certainly will try to show more respect in the future." More often than not, good intentions go unheeded. For our purposes, issues of conflict create opportunities for the small group to evaluate the group covenant. With proper evaluation from time to time, we can ask the question, "Is there a component or element in our group life that needs to be clarified?" or "In what way could we prevent this particular conflict from happening again?"

The conflict, on the other hand, may have nothing to do with the group covenant as much as strong personalities or contrasting beliefs between a couple of people. Perhaps it surfaces with the need for timely admonishment, one of our attributes for creating authentic community. Whatever the case, an opportunity presents itself for accountability with the individuals involved and the resulting resolution.

As we revisit the attributes for creating authentic Christian community, we are reminded how important the getting to know one another, the self-disclosure part of group life, can be. Yet, getting too close for comfort may occur as we move from knowing one another to loving one another in God's love. As we pray that God will help us love and accept others in our group (as they might do concerning us) we learn more about God's will for each of us, particularly during a time of conflict. "Speaking the truth in love..." (Ephesians 4:15) is the reminder that when the proper trust level develops, group members are willing and sometimes eager to enter into confrontation concerning significant matters of life and faith. Truth and love are important ingredients in developing caring relationships. Truth and love develop integrity; a necessary quality for Christian living.

Along with the agreement to disagree and through the healthy process of listening to one another, Augsburger makes the following suggestions concerning the use of pronouns. Following his suggestions, the environment of truth, love, respect, and trust is created. When we express our feelings to another, with whom we may be experiencing conflict, "I" messages are honest, clear, confessional, own my anger, my responsibility, my demands without placing blame. Utilizing "You" messages contrast between honest confession, attack, and distorted rejection. These expressions often create a defensive response.

"I" Messages	"You" Messages
I am angry.	You make me angry.
I feel rejected.	You're judging and rejecting me.
I don't like the wall between us.	You're building a wall between us.
I don't like blaming or being blamed.	You're blaming everything on me.
I want the freedom to say yes or no.	You're trying to run my life.
I want respectful friendship with you again	You've got to respect me or you're not my friend.[82]

It becomes obvious when we read these comments that personalizing our feelings and assumptions is less damaging than the crossfire of blame. Other words to remember to take out of our vocabulary might be; you always, and you never, or there you go again! We can be both loving and angry at the same time, so pick your words wisely.

Using the personal pronoun also allows both sides of you to be expressed. If we are willing to take a risk, be open with our negatives (honest anger) and our positives (affirming love), then the truism that says there are two sides to

---

82 Augsburger, 42.

every story is in place. The situation is now not an attack, but a desire to see understanding and resolution. If small group life includes caring, growing, and doing, the caring part is critical for the healthy life of the group. Caring comes before confrontation and is instrumental in developing love and trust resulting in healthy confrontation or admonishment when the time is right.

DIFFICULT PERSONALITIES

Whenever you have a group of people coming together for discussion, often the only facet unifying the group is Jesus. There is bound to be a variety of personalities represented, each wanting to be heard, or not heard, in various ways, causing a certain amount of friction. The important issue is to anticipate this happening and have a game plan before it begins to ruin the life of the group.

Keep in mind the stages of group life as you travel around the bases of authentic spiritual community. There will be times when diverse personalities will cause frustration. As you lead your group, take time to understand each personality and the various helpful communication skills that will prevent much of the conflict bound to happen. Group diversity is a gift. A small group comprised of ten to twelve people all possessing similar personalities would result in a less than stimulating discussion. The following list identifies the assortment of personalities you might experience in your group. Some are detrimental; some are advantageous, each allowing the group to grow and learn together.

Detrimental	Characteristics
Silent Sarah	Sits silently not entering conversation
Monopolizer Mike	Always first to answer; dominates
Argumentative Angie	Tends to "belittle" other's comment
Tangent Tom	Fast to get conversation off track
Authoritative Arthur	Quickly corrects people; thinks he is right

Advantageous	Characteristics
Clarifier Clark	Ability to clear up confusion in discussion
Encouraging Esther	Expresses appreciation to what's been said
Mediator Molly	Creates harmony during potential conflict
Synthesizer Sam	Able to summarize different viewpoints
Proposer Pete	Initiates ideas and keeps things moving

When leaders are not prepared to tackle difficult personalities, these personalities have a way of creeping in to control the group. The first meeting or two will determine the future patterns of group behavior. It is therefore important to recognize the potential onset of group destruction. Knowing a few communication skills helps with the process of prevention and correction and will assist our response to personalities that tend to sabotage healthy group process.

HEALTHY COMMUNICATION

1. ATTENDING

Attending involves active listening where eye contact and body posture reflect an interest in what the person is saying. "It is more than merely listening to the words. It involves absorbing the content, noting gestures and subtle changes in voice or expressions, and sensing underlying messages."[83] It is discouraging for a group member to participate in the discussion when the leader looks at his or her watch, shuffles papers, or focuses on something other than the person talking. It sends a message of disinterest or insignificant content. Always pay attention to the person speaking, being aware what your body language might be saying. Do not be thinking of your response at the expense of hearing their input. Be creative in affirming their contribution.

In the case of Silent Sarah, the leader should maintain eye contact in order to encourage her to participate in the discussion. Sitting across the circle or table from the silent person helps to achieve this. Having a quiet person week after week warrants taking a moment to speak to the person outside of group time. It is here that the leader has a good opportunity to encourage participation.

On the other hand, sitting next to and not making eye contact with Monopolizer Mike will help to keep him more quiet. Now the leader can break the guideline of eye contact with active listening. Allowing a group member to dominate each week is discouraging to other members and eventually creates unhealthy conflict. Speaking to Monopolizer Mike outside group time can be effective if the leader includes themselves with suggestions such as, "We tend to answer too many questions," or "Let's try to only answer a couple of times this week to see if the rather quiet members will contribute more easily."

---

83 Marianne Schneider Corey and Gerald Corey, Group Process and Practice (Pacific Grove: Brooks/Cole Publishing, 1992), 21.

Remember to be affirmative in approaching this talkative person by commenting on the value of his answers, otherwise he will feel unappreciated.

Think about introducing a question with a comment such as, "Let's hear from someone who hasn't commented tonight," and proceed to ask the question. Now you have encouraged the more quiet person and sent a message to the dominator that it's time for new input. Keep in mind that when the group designs a covenant, one of the goals is that everyone participates in the discussions. It is here that the leader stresses the importance that no one dominates discussion, there are no dumb answers, and everyone has valuable contributions to make. Dominators do come in handy, however, as there may be times when silence reigns and the leader might have to make eye contact with the talkative person to get some discussion going.

2. RE-DIRECTING

Re-directing is a valuable tool for getting focus off the leader and inviting dialogue from other group members. In the initial stages of group life, dialogue generally goes back and forth between leader and a particular member. Remember small group leaders function best as facilitators. It is here that leaders have an opportunity to involve others in the discussion by asking questions such as, "What do the rest of you think about this?" or "How would someone else respond to this question?" Now more of the group is engaged, perhaps even the more silent person. Although it is generally not wise to call on people too early in the life of the group, when trust is apparent and you know the person has worthy input, you should encourage the more quiet person rather than answer yourself.

If Argumentative Angie attempts to make a case for her complaints, or if Authoritative Arthur tries to prove he is the theological expert, asking the question, "Do the rest of you agree with these statements? If so, why?" creates an opening for more inclusive dialogue. For leaders who have the gift of teaching, this is a hard guideline to follow! How leaders love to jump into the discussion and expound on what they have read or experienced over the years. Too much input can, however, become a disservice to group members by stifling significant contributions they might offer. The exception to this would apply if the small group has been designed for the purpose of discipleship and intentional teaching.

Re-directing is also important when Tangent Tom gets off on one of his "This reminds me of a time when …" comments. Although many times there is value in this type of input, more often than not, the story brings the group into differing contexts from the Scripture at hand. It is important not to discourage the tangent person, so thank him or affirm where he is going with the conversation, but attempt to get back on track by saying, "This is interesting and needs to be discussed at some point. Why don't we put this subject in the 'parking lot' to be discussed at a future meeting. For the sake of our time, let's get back to the Scripture being discussed." Now the leader has given value to the member's attempted input and assured him that where he was going with the discussion is worth discussing in the future. At this point, the discussion has been taken back to the proper context of the Scripture for further consideration.

3. EXTENDING

Extending adds to the line of thought and provides the opportunity to present missing information. Extending allows for more thorough discussion on a particular topic and opportunities for correcting a possible wrong answer or misinterpretation of the Scripture being studied. It is important to be aware of body language during answers that do not quite meet expectations in order not to discourage group members from giving opinions. Gently ask, "Have we left anything of importance out of our answers?" or "Does anyone want to offer any more insight before we move on from this particular verse?" Rather than answering or adding from personal knowledge, the leader has opened up the discussion for anyone in the group. Remember the importance of not letting shared ignorance enter into the group discussion. These are gentle, tactful ways to verbalize God's truth as a group wanders from the text.

4. JUSTIFICATION

Justification gets focus back to the truth of Scripture and is a helpful tool for self-disclosure. When Authoritative Arthur makes an incorrect or inappropriate comment or interpretation of Scripture, asking questions like, "That's very interesting! Where did you find that in Scripture?" or "Is there a particular reason why you feel Scripture is stating that message?" helps to disclose the truth and authority of Scripture. This type of question also assists in discovering a personal problem that might be influencing the person's comments. For Argumentative Angie these questions help to uncover the reason why she apparently thrives in presenting an argument.

As attentive listeners and discussion facilitators, leader must strive to involve every small group member in healthy dialogue; it creates more ownership of the group and better retention of the material being discussed. Paying attention to the personalities that often become discouraging or detrimental will assist in the healthy life of the group. Fortunately, most small groups include the various advantageous personalities to help achieve the goal of stimulating discussion. To have a few members like Clarifer Clark who nicely clarifies issues; Encouraging Esther who often will encourage other group members; Mediator Molly who compassionately create more harmony during potential disagreement, or Synthesizer Sam who briefly summarizes or paraphrases from time to time, creates an easier environment for healthy discussion. And when the group has a Proposer Pete who loves to initiate ideas and keep the leader and the group on track, we have the gift of a well-balanced group.

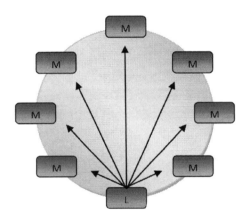

Leader dominates discussion

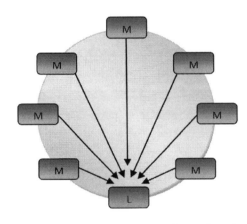

Members direct answers only to leader

When the small group leader makes an effort to involve all the small group members to contribute to the dialogue during the course of the discussion, a healthy situation is created.

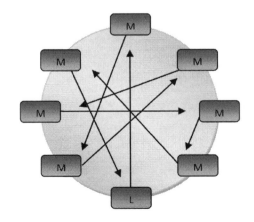

MEDIATION

At times it is necessary to help members in a small group who are experiencing conflict come to resolution. Knowing the rudiments of mediation is necessary in order to guide those involved through the process effectively. One incident I experienced remains vivid in my memory. I knew I was in trouble the moment they walked into my office. "The Awesome Group" had taken a turn for the worse and conflict was destroying our time together. Two young women who had been close friends for some time had had a falling out. The mounting tension was becoming more than the rest of the group was willing to experience. As the group leader, I should have acted sooner.

After speaking with the individuals outside the group gathering, we arranged a time to begin working through this conflict together. Both seemed willing. The boundaries of mediation were set. It was a time to own the conflict at hand, briefly describe the resulting personal turmoil, but not an occasion to reiterate all that had transpired over the several months. The decided goal was an attempt to agree upon a workable solution as to how they could move on. And as they entered my office, I had a sinking feeling this was not going to be successful.

The body language of one young lady was forgiving and the other antagonistic. Forgiving Fran stated her case, apologized and asked for forgiveness for the apparent grief she had caused. Antagonistic Allison's body language said it all as she constantly twitched her crossed leg while madly stirring her coffee; the floor became the object of her focus. There was no apparent acceptance of the request for forgiveness and suddenly the dreaded, "you always... you never... you did." The restricted boundaries of our meeting together had now been broken. I stopped the continuing accusations. Reminding them of the ground rules, I inwardly cried out to God for more of His help. I had prayed so extensively and expected a different outcome. In attempting to find an acceptable solution, I brought the meeting to a close and suggested we have a time of prayer.

Much to my dismay (but should have been predicted) each young woman strongly announced that they were not going to pray. Going to the couch to sit between the two young women, I stated I would pray, but promptly burst into tears. Both women reached out to hug me and affirm the fact that I had tried to solve their problems. I did manage to pray and explain that they both were loved by me and by the group and it was especially sad to see this broken relationship. I sent them out of my office to work things out for themselves. Sitting back in my chair, I felt like a total failure.

Time has passed, both have been guarded with the relationship, but eventually were back to being great friends. It didn't happen overnight. The attempted resolution did help to restore a more amicable relationship, but it was a slow process of trust and acceptance before restoration. This exemplifies the difficulty in conflict while impressing the importance of dealing early with the issue. Perhaps if I had taken the lead earlier, studied a bit more about conflict resolution, we might have prevented much of the grief.

MEDIATION: THE RIGHT PROCESS

"Mediation exists when a neutral and impartial third party assists two or more parties in negotiating a constructive resolution of their conflict. To be successful, mediators need to possess certain characteristics and adopt particular strategies. Mediators need to be perceived as being trustworthy and able. Mediation facilitates conflict resolution in the following ways:

1. Reducing emotional upset by giving parties an opportunity to vent their feelings.
2. Presenting alternative solutions by recasting the issues in different or more acceptable terms.
3. Providing opportunities for "graceful retreat" or face-saving in the eyes of one's adversary, one's constituency, the public, or oneself.
4. Facilitating constructive communication among parties.
5. Controlling contact between the parties, including such aspects as the neutrality of the meeting site, the formality of the setting, the time constraints, and the number and kinds of people at the meeting."[84]

Becoming familiar with these five steps for the mediation process is helpful to leaders in facilitating the small group through the various stages of group life. If the leader senses the emerging presence of conflict, he or she must be willing to recognize the situation, the level of severity, and respond in an effective manner.

There are times when conflict is beyond our experience or capabilities for achieving resolution. It is helpful to create a resource list for more professional

---

84 Adapted from B. Ravin and J. Rubin, Social Psychology: People in Groups (New York: John Wiley, 1976), 462 quoted in Johnson and Johnson, 358-359.

help as the situation might demand. Do not try to carry the burden of individual or group problems when you have limited expertise. Remember that conflict can be healthy and should be expected in the process of Scripture application where truth and life intersect. "Most of our conflicts and difficulties come from trying to deal with the spiritual and practical aspects of our life separately instead of realizing them as parts of one whole."[85]

DEALING WITH COMMON PROBLEMS

1. DEAD SILENCE

Do not panic. People need to think and reflect. Many leaders become anxious and jump into the dialogue with their own answers. If silence prevails, rephrase the question, bring in some humor, and create a comfort level. Making eye contact with the monopolizer is the last resource. Utilize communication skills. Saying, "I know all of you have many wonderful thoughts and ideas concerning this Scripture. Come on, let's hear them!" will create a more encouraging atmosphere for group participation. Expect more silence in the early stages of group life.

2. STARTING AND ENDING ON TIME

Beginning late and ending late develops a problematic pattern that creates tension and uncertainty. Be a good gatekeeper with the time, or better still, delegate the responsibility to another group member. Reviewing the covenant to remind members of the decisions concerning the starting and finishing details may be in order. Checking first with the host, the discussion should stop at the designated time, allowing those who need to leave to do so without guilt, and at the same time, invite others to stay for further discussion. You do not need to kill a question through excessive discussion or stop only when there is a lull in the conversation. Leaving the group with high momentum and excitement is an advantage for the next meeting together.

3. THE UNANSWERED QUESTION

Everyone in the small group, leader included, is committed to growing spiritually together. There will be times when leaders will not know the answer

---

85 Evelyn Underhill, The Spiritual Life, quoted in: Ruben Job and Norman Shawchuck, 315.

to a particular question. Do not be afraid to say "I do not know, but I certainly will try to find the answer this week for you." Find the answer during the week, or better still, delegate the responsibility to someone else in the group. The term shared ignorance has been mentioned throughout this training on healthy small group process, and it is critical that leaders do not allow inaccurate interpretations to prevail. Guessing or stating an answer that sounds good is not acceptable.

4. THE INGROWN OR STALE GROUP

When the small group appears to become boring, less effective in caring or growing together, take time to involve the group in healthy evaluation. Important to this evaluation is revisiting the covenant for stated goals and purposes for your time together. What components of healthy small group life have been omitted? Would this be a good time to include mission and outreach within your church or community? What options for mission do you have? In what way would opening the group to new people bring fresh and creative interaction? What has worked well and where could the group improve? Is it time for the group to multiply and help to expand the small group ministry? If so, what way will be the most effective?

Honest evaluation of group life is essential. At some point, every group comes to an end and ending well is important. Two years with the same group can be quite effective. Adding a third year without making changes or adding appropriate mission often results in ineffective group life. Jesus set the example in leading his small group for three years, but notice that during that time of discipleship, the disciples were sent out to do mission and act upon what they had learned (Matthew 10). Recognize the time to make changes before the group experience becomes too routine.

5. EXTRA CARE PERSON

There are those times when the well-prepared group meeting will change dramatically. When a group member experiences pain, stop and allow time for special care and prayer. A problem arises, however, when this particular person has expectations for special attention each week. This repetition often destroys the enthusiasm of the group members. Taking time to pray for the extra care person is necessary and important. Rather than continuing large segments of group time to address this problem, suggest finding a time during the week to get together and continue the dialogue. During this additional meeting, it is important to set boundaries for group sharing in order to retain the healthy environment for the rest of the small group. Do not let the needy member control the life of the group each week. Love, care, and compassion should be experienced within your group life but, if this is abused, group members will become discouraged and attrition will result.

On the other hand, learn to recognize when a group member has serious problems. When the emotionally needy person is identified, a leader must consider the special needs this person has and whether the group as a whole can provide the care this person requires. It would be wise to talk to the staff overseeing the small group ministry, or talk privately to the particular person. Small group leaders usually are not trained professional counselors and the group is not designed as a therapy group. As difficult as it is, the leader might need to explain to the member that the group apparently is not the right place for him or her at that time. Critical in this process is to find help for the "extra care" member as a reminder that they are loved and valuable as a child of God.

Problems surface in the best of small group experiences. Consider various options for managing the difficult times due to situations and personalities that cause friction, and ultimately unhealthy conflict. Remember to deal with them quickly as patterns get established early in the group life. Concerning the difficult personalities, the goal should be to find out what is behind the unhealthy behavior. In any case, understanding the characteristics and thwarting their dominance will increase the health of your group.

SCRIPTURE TO CONSIDER:

- » Speak the truth in love (Ephesians 4:15).
- » In your anger, do not sin (Ephesians 4:26).
- » Forgive whatever grievances you have (Colossians 3:13).
- » Do not keep a record of wrongs (1 Corinthians 13:5).
- » Do not pay evil for evil, insult for insult (1 Peter 3:8).
- » Be kind and compassionate, forgiving each other (Ephesians 4:32).
- » Do what leads to peace and mutual edification (Romans 14:19).
- » Do not slander one another (James 4:11).
- » Live in harmony with one another (Romans 12:16).
- » Above all, love one another deeply (1 Peter 4:4).

As small group leaders, we will experience various emotions. There are times of great anticipation, excitement, achievement, creativity, and satisfaction. Yet we will also experience a sense of failure, frustration, inadequacy, and disappointment. Nevertheless, the huge impact intentional leadership can make in individuals and within the church community is an awesome privilege. Considering and acting upon an intentional leadership role that results in healthy small group life will assist in providing environments for life-change. Commit to developing authentic Christian community through honest risk taking and truth telling, through times of confession and reconciliation, and through the experience of knowing, loving, serving, admonishing, and celebrating.

TOO CLOSE FOR COMFORT

1. DISCUSS

In what way have you identified with the two case studies of conflict presented in this chapter? Identify your style of confrontation. Discuss how this chapter has been helpful in understanding your strategy. Describe insights that will assist you with difficult personalities. Are there additional skills you use for conflict resolution that would be helpful to share? Briefly describe.

Role-playing is useful for experiencing concepts and skills. The designated leader for this chapter study prepares this activity. Select from the following personality descriptors, (add additional roles if needed), and write on a slip of paper the role and expectations. Each member draws a role without disclosing their assignment and attempts to respond to questions or discussion with the corresponding characteristics of that particular personality. The leader will need to recall some of the responses necessary to overcome potential conflict presented by these frequent difficult personalities. A few advantageous personalities are included to help the leader with the healthy process. Role-playing reinforces the valuable and appropriate responses every effective discussion leader needs to know. Work into the roles slowly, but emphatically and have fun!

The role definitions should read as follows:

- » **Leader:** Lead the following Bible study. As members play their roles, attempt to utilize the various skills and responses you have learned to the selected personalities as you facilitate the discussion.
- » **Monopolizer Mike:** Slowly, but eagerly, begin to answer most of the questions.
- » **Argumentative Angie:** Respond to group member's answers as if they were not quite good enough: e.g. "Well, I don't think you really have experienced this type of stress."
- » **Tangent Tom:** Jump into a discussion with comments like: "This reminds me of a time when … " or, "This really isn't applicable, but let me tell you … !"
- » **Authoritative Arthur:** Be eager to correct a member's interpretation or understanding of Scripture: e.g. "Actually, the Scripture does not imply that, but…" or "I've studied this many times and I'm not hearing the

right responses tonight." You might mention all the concordances you have consulted.

» **Clarifying Clark:** Try to clear up any confusing comments between two or more members. You might say: "What I hear Jack saying is a bit different from what I think you, Sam, think he is saying."

» **Encouraging Esther:** Express appreciation for input that others have contributed. An occasional: "Kara, I really appreciate your comments. They are helpful to me. Thanks!"

» **Proposer Pete:** Create some new energy by making constructive suggestions such as: "I think our group is ready to do some mission. Am I right?" or "I think we've about exhausted our resources on this topic. We should move on."

Having assigned the personalities to be played, role-play the Bible study discussion.

2. TELL

» Think of a time when conflict with someone seemed to rule your life. Briefly describe one or two emotions and responses you experienced. In what way was the conflict resolved?

» Have you experienced letting someone else down in a significant way? If so, briefly describe the feelings that you experienced.

» Has there been a time when given a perfect opportunity to share Christ, you failed to speak? Thinking about the incident at a later time, what were your emotions?

THREE STRIKES AND YOU'RE OUT?

Read John 21:15-19

3. SCRIPTURE

To prepare for this Bible study, please read Mark 14:27-31; Luke 22:31-34; Luke 22:54-62, and Matthew 16:17. Understanding the earlier experience of Peter may help to reinforce the significance of this Scripture.

It was the third time Jesus had revealed himself to his disciples after he was raised from the dead. Seven disciples and Jesus are now sharing a breakfast of freshly caught fish on the Sea of Galilee shore. Jesus' attention is focused on Peter.

Look (observation)

» What questions does Jesus ask Peter? What are the significant words? How did Jesus address Peter?
» What were Peter's responses? Apparent emotions?

Think (interpretation)

» Pretend you are Peter. What comes to mind when you hear Jesus' questions three times? What might be the object of Peter's love other than Jesus?
» What is Jesus charging Peter to do?
» Was the repetition necessary? Why or why not?
» What does Jesus imply by using the words he chooses?
» Why does Jesus reveal the sort of death Peter might experience? Why do you think Jesus brought the topic into the conversation?

Act (application)

» "Feed" and "tend" are significant imperatives and should be considered carefully. Do these words apply to us? If so, as a small group leader, in what way are you able and willing to fulfill these mandates?
» Jesus ends the conversation with "follow me." What does that look like for you?
» Is there an area of your life that needs to be reconciled to Jesus? If so, what one step will you take to make it right?
» If Jesus was publicly forgiving and reinstating Peter for Peter's confidence, what principle from this lesson might apply to you? In what way?
» Reconciliation is at the heart of the gospel of Jesus Christ. Is there someone with whom you need to be reconciled? Is there someone with whom you have reconciled but would benefit from your encouragement and confidence? What step will you take this week to blend your belief and your behavior and go to that person with the love of Christ?

Think back again to Peter and the night he betrayed Jesus by denying three times that he was one of Jesus' disciples. Peter's soul agonized in his failure to love Jesus openly. Peter wept bitterly (Luke 22:62). Evidently three strikes for Peter and he was not out for John 21:15-19 records Jesus' reinstatement of Peter. Jesus three times asked Peter if he loved him. Peter responds three times and says he does! Jesus challenged Peter with the tremendous task of overseeing spiritual care and all that the care would imply for the newly form-ing church.

A small group leader is called to be a care-giver and a shepherd to a small group of people yearning for spiritual care, connection, and meaningful rela-tionships. Committing to this strategic role is a privilege of leadership, and we do so because we also love Jesus and stand forgiven. As Jesus challenged Peter, he expects us to take our leadership responsibilities seriously. In the name of Jesus, we become trusted, vulnerable, reliable, and Spirit-filled leaders; offering friendship, encouragement, confidence, and hope to those in our groups.

4. PRAYER

As a small group leader, you have spent eight weeks discovering and review-ing the Scriptural basis, concepts, skills, case studies, and challenges in eight areas of small group process. The training goals and intentions of Renewing Your Church Through Healthy Small Groups have been to provide tools and information that will help you lead with excellence as you create arenas for life-transformation. Are there aspects of leadership that concern you? Take time to pray with one another expressing your concerns as you begin or con-tinue your responsibility as a small group leader. And, may the power of the Holy Spirit enable you to do what God has placed in your hands.

"Therefore, as God's chosen people, holy and dearly loved, clothe yourselves with compassion, kindness, humility, gentleness and patience. Bear with each other and forgive whatever grievances you may have against one another. Forgive as the Lord forgave you. And over all these virtues put on love, which binds them all together in perfect unity. Let the peace of Christ rule in your hearts, since as members of one body you were called to peace. And be thankful. Let the word of Christ dwell in you richly as you teach and admonish one another with all wisdom, and as you sing psalms, hymns and spiritual songs with gratitude in your hearts to God. And whatever you do, whether in word or deed, do it all in the name of the Lord Jesus, giving thanks to God the Father through him."

Colossians 3:12-17

CONCLUSION

THE HOPE OF RENEWAL

*"So I prophesied as he commanded me,
and breath entered them; they came to life
and stood up on their on their feet—a vast army."*

Ezekiel 37:10

When God created the nation of Israel, He gave them a covenant, the Mosaic covenant, as their constitution. For the people of God, the covenant was not a collection of laws to burden them, rather, statutes and commandments for what God expected from His people for their own good, allowing them to receive the promised blessings. God expected obedience from His people. Israel, however, continued to live in disobedience. As part of God's discipline, the nation of Israel experienced suppression and dispersion. It was part of God's plan to bring Israel back to Him.

Ezekiel, as a watchman for Israel, spoke to his contemporaries declaring not only the coming judgment of God, but the holiness of God, His faithfulness, and continued love for them. Through this steadfast love, God would one day cleanse and restore the nation of Israel to a forgiven nation; a nation that would serve God as the one true God. Restoration and hope is a major theme throughout this prophetical book of the Old Testament. It is during this period of hope that Ezekiel experiences a vision that gave encouragement to a scattered nation, hope for the future restoration, and the coming messianic kingdom.

In this vision, a prophecy was given to Ezekiel concerning restoration as he was led throughout a devastated valley of countless dry bones. "Son of man, can these bones live?" God asked. "O Sovereign Lord, you alone know," replied Ezekiel (Ezekiel 37:3-4). God then responded to Ezekiel:

Prophesy to these bones and say to them, 'Dry bones, hear the word of the Lord! This is what the Sovereign Lord says to these bones: I will make breath enter you, and you will come to life. I will attach tendons to you and make flesh come upon you and cover you with skin; I will put breath in you, and you will come to life. Then you will know that I am the Lord' (Ezekiel 37:4-6).

And now a miracle developed as tendons, flesh, and skin came upon the dry bones. But no breath was found in them, so Ezekiel was instructed by God to prophesy once more.

Prophesy to the breath; prophesy, son of man, and say to it, 'This is what the Sovereign Lord says: Come from the four winds, O breath, and breathe into these slain, that they may live.' So I prophesied as he commanded me, and breath entered them; they came to life and stood up on their feet—a vast army (Ezekiel 37:9-10).

This time breath was commanded to enter into these reconstructed, lifeless bodies. As breath permeated each body, Ezekiel stood in amazement as an army of people came alive! The "breath" (wind or Spirit) portrayed the spiritual renewal of God's people.

Ezekiel's vision gave immediate hope to the nation of Israel. As exiles, this chosen nation of God longed to return to their home land. The vision was a picture of resurrection and restoration, and most certainly a renewed relationship with the one true God. Yahweh would be their God and they would be His people.

Today's culture reflects a "valley of dry bones." People have turned from biblical truth to relative truth where each decides what is right and wrong in their own eyes. The gospel is not preached in many worship services. Belief in a loving, personal God waivers. God's Word takes a back seat to pragmatic behavior. Organizations commit to dissolve laws, traditions, and visibility of Christian mindsets and celebrations. Today the people of God need a vision of dry bones coming to life.

In what way can healthy small groups bring the breath of life into the dry bones of our churches and our communities? Certainly healthy small groups are not the only answer, yet striving to create environments where people are personally known, feel loved and accepted, served and cared for, challenged and held accountable, honored and celebrated, provide opportunities for God's Word to be explored and acted upon in a safe and trusting community of friends. It is here where God can breathe anew His Spirit into lives that are dry and lifeless. It is here that God's Word can shape and reshape attitudes and actions that displease Him. It is here that hope, security, and the steadfast love of God gives redemption and new life. It is here where God can renew individuals, and therefore the church.

As a small group leader, you may have a part in introducing dry bones to the breath of life. It is a strategic role in the church today. Growing in Christian character and learning and practicing the skills for creating healthy small group environments assist people on to God's agenda and spiritual renewal; to be imitators of Christ and to become what God originally intended. Being committed to create authentic communities, to lead with excellence, to design groups with goals and purposes, to worship together, to study the Bible with integrity, to create life-changing relationships and dialogues, and to resolve impending conflict in ways that honor God, are stepping stones for renewal. Yes, God can build intentional relationships for life-transformation and spiritually renew your church today through authentic Christian communities; the healthy small group!

It is easily forgotten that the fellowship of Christian brethren is a gift of grace, a gift of the kingdom of God that any day may be taken from us, that the time that still separates us from utter loneliness may be brief indeed. Therefore, let him who until now has had the privilege of living a common Christian life with other Christians praise God's grace from the bottom of his heart. Let him thank God on his knees and declare: It is grace, nothing but grace, that we are allowed to live in community with Christian brethren."[86]

---

86 Dietrich Bonhoffer, Life Together, (HarperSanFrancisco, 1954), 20.

APPENDIX

EVALUATING YOUR GROUP

*"Quality small groups will not happen
without formal evaluation."*

Neal McBride, *How to Lead Small Groups*

Throughout this training, the importance of the five essential attributes for creating healthy, authentic Christian community have been identified and explored: knowing, loving, serving, admonishing, and celebrating. Taking time to examine and evaluate these attributes allows for adjustment and refinement in the group life and expectations. Implementing necessary changes must be part of the group process in order to not only continue the established goals and purposes for the group's existence, but to implement changes that spur one another on to intimate communion with God, deeper relationships with one another, and a growing dependence on the Holy Spirit for glorifying God in life and practice.

The idea of personal evaluation is clearly mandated in Scripture. King David cried out to God: "Test me, O Lord, and try me, examine my heart and my mind" (Psalm 26:2). The apostle Paul warns: "Examine yourselves to see whether you are in the faith; test yourselves" (2 Corinthians 13:5a). The writer of the book of Hebrews states: "The word of God is living and active. Sharper than any double-edged sword, it penetrates even to dividing soul and spirit, joints and marrow; it judges the thoughts and attitudes of the heart. Nothing in all creation is hidden from God's sight. Everything is uncovered and laid bare before the eyes of him to whom we must give account" (Hebrews 4:12-13).

None of these verses are in the context of evaluating an existing small group, but the principle of evaluation is clearly stated. Center to the concept of evaluation is the idea of accountability, and being accountable to God and one another should be a significant goal for small group meetings. So with this concept in mind, it is necessary to consider evaluation, the barriers within the process of evaluation a group leader might encounter, and the benefits of achieving a process that not only meets the needs of the small group, but strengthens the quality of group life and learning. "On-going evaluation promotes quality, builds in accountability, and provides the basis for making responsible decisions."[87]

Evaluation is often not well received with small group members. Perhaps it is an element of threat concerning the comfort level, the idea of change, or an aversion to possible confrontation. It is advantageous for the group leader to consider these possibly reactions small group members have concerning group evaluation. Be sensitive and patient as you begin the process of group evaluation.

Throughout each of the preceding chapters, the need for evaluation has been stressed. Evaluation is a tool; it is not a guarantee that the small group will solve all of its problems, if they exist, but will be an important catalyst for creating authentic Christian community and improving the health of the small group. Assisting group members in understanding the value of evaluation helps to address individual fears, reinforce vision, and develops stronger ownership of the group life together. The construction of a well-defined and realistic covenant is critical to the process. Subjects of evaluation should include the details of the group's format; the developing relationships; the accountability to God, others, the church, and the outward acts of grace and mercy.

It is human hesitancy to avoid critique or affirmation in the context of the small group. This keeps group members at a distance from one another. It impairs the vulnerability the group should experience. Different groups need more or less evaluation. In the beginning stages of group life, evaluations should occur more frequently for the health of the group. As the group matures, evaluation is helpful after ending a study, when a person leaves the group, or if a crisis has happened. In the summer, every small group should change their format from the on-going routine. Always end your time together with an evaluation and set new ideas and the implementation in place before taking a break. Celebrate your time together!

Using the covenant as a guide, evaluation of the group's on-going experience

---

87 Neal McBride, How to Lead Small Groups (NavPress: Colorado Springs, 1990), 120-121. Quote is abbreviated.

can be summarized by basically asking one valuable, simple question: "What has worked and what has not?" If times of evaluations are not intentionally planned, they will not happen correctly; they will be done either in private or be unspoken. A healthy small group evaluates their experiences and allows opportunities for the freedom of personal expression in a trusting environment. This evaluation process is instrumental in developing an authentic Christian community where, by God's grace, spiritual renewal and life-transformation happens.

Evaluation Tool

The leadership of the evaluation time is strategically important. The group leader, or a group member, who leads evaluation events should be well-prepared in advance, anticipating issues, concerns, hidden agendas, and broken relationships. The facilitator of the evaluation needs to be a person of patience and prayer who understands the dynamics of group process and conflict resolution as well thought-out evaluations will reveal concerns and conflicts may arise. Evaluation without strong leadership could shatter a weak or wavering group. Consider the following suggestions for your evaluation time:

- » In reviewing our covenant, have we allotted adequate time for the essential ingredients of nurture, worship, community building, and mission? If not, what necessary changes need to be made?
- » What do we like about our group?
- » In what way has this group met our expectations?
- » How have we shown concern and affection for one another?
- » How well have we learned to share truthfully and deeply the things that really matter in life?
- » In what way can we improve our group life together?
- » In what way has our faith grown since we joined this small group?
- » Briefly describe a fulfilling moment during our time together.
- » Talk about a time when you felt frustrated with being part of this group.
- » What group behaviors would we like to change? Encourage?
- » What is the quality of our group sharing, reflection, and prayer? In what ways does this reflect going around the bases of small group life?
- » How often have we experienced answered prayer?
- » How committed are we to praying for one another, getting together with one another, or serving one another outside of group time?
- » How often do we pray for those who do not know Christ?

- » In what way are we involved in mission and outreach?
- » Should our group consider an outreach event? What would that look like?
- » In what way does our group support the life of the church?
- » Are there reasons for us to consider changing our open or closed status? Identify and discuss reasons.
- » How successful are we in spiritual accountability to one another?
- » How could we make the accountability application segment of our Bible study stronger?
- » In what way have we acknowledged and utilized the spiritual gifts of our group members?
- » How have we helped in identifying potential small group leaders?
- » Should we consider multiplying our group? Why or why not?
- » How have we celebrated and affirmed one another? In what way have we felt comfortable admonishing one another?
- » What one change in your life are you celebrating because you were part of this small group?

BIBLIOGRAPHY

Almstrom, Sidney D. A Religious History of the American People. New Haven: Yale University Press, 1972.

Arnold, Jeffrey. The Big Book on Small Groups. Downers Grove: InterVarsity Press, 1992.

_____. Discovering the Bible for Yourself. Downers Grove: Intervarsity Press, 1993.

Augsberger, David. Caring Enough to Confront. Ventura: Regal Books, 1973.

Barker, Steve, Judy Johnson, Jimmy Long, Rob Malone, and Ron Nicholas. Small Group Leaders Guide. Downers Grove: InterVarsity Press, 1982.

_____. Judy Johnson, Rob Malone, Ron Nicholas, and Doug Whallon. Good Things Come in Small Groups. Downers Grove: Intervarsity Press, 1985.

Blackaby, Henry and Richard Blackaby. Spiritual Leadership. Nashville: Broadman and Holman, 2001.

Bonhoeffer, Dietrich. Life Together. New York: HarperCollins Publishing, 1954.

Cedar, Paul. The Life of Prayer. Nasville: Word, 1998.

Cho, Dr. Paul Y. Successful Home Cell Groups. South Plainfield: Bridge, 1960.

Clinton, Robert. The Making of a Leader. Colorado Springs: NavPress, 1988.

Cloud, Henry, and John Townsend. Making Small Groups Work. Grand Rapids: Zondervan, 2003.

Corey, Maianne Schneider, and Gerald Corey. Groups Process and Practice. 4th ed. Pacific Grove: Brooks/Cole Publishing, 1992.

Comiskey, Joel. Leadership Explosion. Houston: Touch, 2000.

Crabb, Larry. The Safest Place on Earth. Nashville: Word, 1999.

Dibbert, Michael, and Frank Wichern. Growth Groups. Grand Rapids: Zondervan, 1985.

Donahue, Bill. Leading Life Changing Small Groups. Grand Rapids: Zondervan, 1996.

_____, and Russ Robinson. Building a Church of Small Groups. Grand Rapids: Zondervan, 2001.

_____. Seven Deadly Sins of Small Group Ministry. Grand Rapids: Zondervan, 2002.

_____. Walking the Small Group Tightrope. Grand Rapids: Zondervan, 2003.

Drummond, Lewis A. Reaching Generation Next. Grand Rapids: Baker Books, 2002.

Eims, Leroy. Be A Motivational Leader. Wheaton: Victor Books, 1982.

Fee, Gordon, and Douglas Stuart. How to Read the Bible for All Its Worth. Grand Rapids: Zondervan, 1983.

Ferlo, Roger. Opening the Bible. Cambridge, Massachusetts: Cowley Press, 1997.

Fisher, Roger, William Ury, and Bruce Patton. Getting to Yes. 2nd ed. New York: Penguin Books, 1991.

Finzel, Hans. The Top Ten Mistakes Leaders Make. Colorado Springs: Victor Books, 1994.

_____. Opening The Book. Colorado Springs: Victor Books, 1972,

Ford, Leighton. The Power of the Story. Colorado Springs: NavPress, 1994.

Foster, Richard J. Prayer. San Francisco: Harper, 1982.

_____. Celebration of Discipline. San Francisco: Harper & Row, 1978.

George, Carl. Prepare Your Church For The Future. Grand Rapids: Flemming H. Revell Co., 1992.

_____. Nine Keys to Effective Small Group Leadership. Mansfield, Pennsylvania: Kingdom Publishing, 1971.

Gire, Ken. The Reflective Life. Colorado Springs: Chariot Victor, 1998.

Griffin, Em. Getting Together. Downers Grove: InterVarsity Press, 1982.

Gorman, Julie A. Community That Is Christian. Wheaton: Victor Books, 1993.

Haller, William. The Rise of Puritanism. 2nd ed. Philadelphia: University of Pennsylvania Press, 1984.

Hambrick-Stowe, Charles. E. The Practice of Piety. Chapel Hill: University of North Carolina Press, 1982.

Haugk, Kenneth. Christian Caregiving. Minneapolis: Augsburg Publishing House, 1984.

Henderson, Michael D. John Wesley's Class Meetings. Nappanee, Indiana: Asbury, 1997.

Hestenes, Roberta. Using The Bible In Groups. Philadelphia: The Westminster Press, 1983.

_____. Turning Committees into Communities. Colorado: NavPress, 1991.

Icenogle, Gareth. Biblical Foundations For Small Group Ministry. Downers Grove: InterVarsity, 1994.

Johnson, David W. and Frank P. Johnson. Joining Together. Needham Heights: Allyn and Bacon, 1991.

Johnson, Jan. When the Soul Listens. Colorado Springs: NavPress, 1999.

Kuhatschek, Jack. Applying the Bible, Downers Grove: InterVarsity Press, 1990.

Latourette, Kenneth Scott. A History of Christianity: Reformation to the Present. San Francisco: Harper, 1975.

Lee-Thorp, Karen. How To Ask Great Questions. Colorado Springs: NavPress, 1998.

Lovelace, Richard F. Renewal as a Way of Life. Downers Grove: InterVarsity Press, 1985.

Macchia, Stephen A. Becoming A Healthy Church. Grand Rapids: Baker Books, 1999.

_____. Becoming a Healthy Disciple. Grand Rapids: Baker Books, 2004.

Maxwell, John C. The 21 Indispensable Qualities of a Leader. Nashville: Nelson Books, 1999.

McBride, Neal. How To Lead Small Groups. Colorado Springs: NavPress, 1990.

McGrath, Alister E. Spirituality in an Age of Change. Grand Rapids: Zondervan, 1994.

McIntosh, Gary L. One Church Four Generations. Grand Rapids: Baker Books, 2002.

Nouwen, Henry. In the Name of Jesus. New York: Crossroads, 1994.

_____. The Wounded Healer. New York: Image, 1972.

_____. Life of the Beloved. New York: Crossroad, 1993.

Nyquist, James, and Jack Kuhatschek. Leading Bible Studies. Downers Grove: InterVarsity Press, 1985.

Plueddemann, Jim, and Carol Plueddemann. Pilgrims in Progress. Wheaton: Shaw, 1990.

Portaro, Sam. Conflict and a Christian Life. Cambridge, Massachusetts: Cowley Publications, 2003.

Rinehart, Stacy T. Upside Down. Colorado Springs: NavPress, 1998.

Sande, Ken. The Peace Maker. Grand Rapids: Baker Books, 1991.

Sire, James W. Scripture Twisting. Downers Grove: InterVarsity Press, 1980.

Sproul, R.C. Knowing Scripture. Downers Grove: InterVarsity Press, 1977.

Stark, Rodney. The Rise of Christianity. San Francisco: HarperCollins, 1996.

Stott, John R. W. Your Mind Matters. Grand Rapids: InterVarsity Press, 1982.

Swindoll, Charles R. Dropping Your Guard. Waco: Word Books, 1983.

Swartz, Christian A. Natural Church Development. 6th ed. St. Charles, Illinois: ChurchSmart Resources, 2003.

Thrall, Bill, Bruce McNicol, and Ken McElrath. The Ascent of a Leader. San Francisco: Jossey-Bass, 1999.

Williams, Dan. Seven Myths About Small Groups. Downers Grove: InterVarsity Press, 1991.

Wuthnow, Robert. Sharing the Journey. New York: The Free Press, 1994.

Coursework

Hestenes, Roberta. "Building Christian Community through Small Groups." Fuller Theological Seminary, Pasadna, California, 1994.

Peace, Richard. "Pursuit of Wholeness." Gordon-Conwell Theological Seminary, South Hamilton, Massachusetts, 1995.

Robinson, Haddon. "Communicating the Scriptures to a Modern World." Gordon-Conwell Theological Seminary, South Hamilton, Massachusetts, 1993.

ABOUT THE AUTHOR

Diana Curren Bennett, D.Min.

Diana received the Master of Arts of Theological Studies from Gordon-Conwell Theological Seminary, Hamilton, Massachusetts, in 1996 and received the Doctor of Ministry: Ministry in the New England Context degree, 2006. She holds two certificates in Spiritual Direction and is a licensed minister with the Conservative Congregational Christian Conference.

Diana has worked with church small group ministries for many years. In 1980 she formed a Community Bible Study chapter where she trained small group leaders, served as Area Director and Teaching Director. In 1990 she became Director of Small Groups, South Shore Baptist Church, Hingham, Massachusetts, and in 1994 Minister of Small Groups, Park Street Church, Boston, Massachusetts. During this time she also served as a small group leadership trainer for the Pilgrimage Training Group and eventually created a small group leadership training seminar from personal knowledge and experience including resources that lend themselves to developing healthy small group process. In 2000 Diana became Director of Small Group Ministries for Vision New England, Acton, Massachusetts and in 2003 joined Leadership Transformations, Inc. (LTI) where she served as Director of Emmaus: Spiritual Leadership Communities for eight years and is presently Director of Ministry Relations. Diana is actively involved as a Bible study teacher and as a Spiritual Director. She lives with her husband in Hingham, Massachusetts, has three married children and a small group of ten grandchildren.

SMALL GROUP MATERIALS FROM LEADERSHIP TRANSFORMATIONS

 Broken and Whole offers the gifts of love found in 1 Corinthians 13 as the antidote to our brokenness. Each chapter concludes with a powerful spiritual assessment tool to use in reflecting on our own leadership strengths and weaknesses. By embracing and befriending our own brokenness we can find true wholeness.

 Crafting a Rule of Life will take you and your small group through the process of creating your own personal rule of life using St. Benedict as a guide. Through the basic disciplines of Scripture, prayer, and reflection this practical workbook will lead your small group on a journey toward Christlikeness.

 **Becoming a Healthy Disciple** explores the ten traits of a healthy disciple, including a vital prayer life, evangelistic outreach, worship, servanthood, and stewardship. Discipleship is a lifelong apprenticeship to Jesus Christ, the master teacher. John the beloved disciple is used as an example of a life lived close to Christ.

 Becoming a Healthy Disciple Small Group Study & Worship Guide is a companion to *Becoming a Healthy Disciple*. This 12-week small group resource provides Study, Worship, and Prayer guidelines for each session working through the ten traits of a healthy disciple.

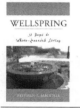 **Wellspring: 31 Days to Whole-Hearted Living** The Bible is filled with more than 50 depictions of the heart, such as hardened, humble, deceitful, and grateful. God's desire is to woo his followers to devote their whole heart to him in all aspects of their personal life and worship: loving God with "all" their heart.

 Path of a Beloved Disciple: 31 Days in the Gospel of John Welcome to the delightful journey of discipleship! Jesus invites us to say an enthusiastic "Yes!" to his beckoning call: Come close, draw near, and follow me. This is exactly what John the Beloved Disciple said long ago and it's our invitation to intimacy today.

 **Outstretched Arms of Grace: A 40 Day Lenten Devotional** This Lenten devotional will take your group through the 40 days of Lent ensuring your hearts are attentive to the gifts of grace that Jesus has given in his ultimate sacrifice on the cross: forgiveness of sins, fullness of life, and a forever home awaiting you in heaven.

Guide to Prayer for All Who Walk With God

The latest from Rueben Job, A Guide to Prayer for All Who Walk With God offers a simple pattern of daily prayer built around weekly themes and organized by the Christian church year. Each week features readings for reflection from such well-known spiritual writers as Francis of Assisi, Teresa of Avila, Dietrich Bonhoeffer, Henri J. M. Nouwen, Sue Monk Kidd, Martin Luther, Julian of Norwich, M. Basil Pennington, Evelyn Underhill, Douglas Steere, and many others.

Guide to Prayer for All Who Seek God

For nearly 20 years, people have turned to the Guide to Prayer series for a daily rhythm of devotion and personal worship. Thousands of readers appreciate the series' simple structure of daily worship, rich spiritual writings, lectionary guidelines, and poignant prayers. Like its predecessors, A Guide to Prayer for All Who Seek God will become a treasured favorite for those hungering for God as the Christian year unfolds.

Guide to Prayer for Ministers and Other Servants

A best-seller for more than a decade! This classic devotional and prayer book includes thematically arranged material for each week of the year as well as themes and schedules for 12 personal retreats. The authors have adopted the following daily format for this prayer book: daily invocations, readings, scripture, reflection, prayers, weekly hymns, benedictions, and printed psalms.

Guide to Prayer for All God's People

A compilation of scripture, prayers and spiritual readings, this inexhaustible resource contains thematically arranged material for each week of the year and for monthly personal retreats. Its contents have made it a sought-after desk reference, a valuable library resource and a cherished companion.

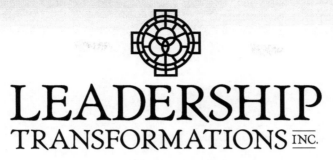

LEADERSHIP
TRANSFORMATIONS INC.

FORMATION | DISCERNMENT | RENEWAL

- Soul Care Retreats and Soul Sabbaths

- Emmaus: Spiritual Leadership Communities

- Selah: Certificate Program in Spiritual Direction (Selah-West, Selah-East)

- Spiritual Formation Groups

- Spiritual Health Assessments

- Spiritual Discernment for Teams

- Sabbatical Planning and Coaching

- Spiritual Formation Resources

Visit www.LeadershipTransformations.org
or call (877) TEAM LTI.

Made in the USA
Columbia, SC
26 August 2017